The Beach Boys On CD: vol 1 - The 1960s

Andrew Hickey

Copyright © Andrew Hickey 2011, all rights reserved. The author has asserted his moral rights.

All song lyrics are copyright their respective owners, and are quoted for review purposes in accordance with fair dealing and fair use laws. No claim over them is asserted.

BY THE SAME AUTHOR:
Sci-Ence! Justice Leak!
The Beatles In Mono

I love my Carl
I love my Brian, my Dennis, and my Al
I can even find it in my heart to love Mike Love
I Love My Car, Belle & Sebastian

For Holly

Contents

Acknowledgements	7
Introduction	9
Surfin' Safari/Surfin' USA	13
Surfin' Safari	14
Surfin' USA	19
CD Bonus Tracks	24
Surfer Girl/Shut Down Vol. 2	25
Surfer Girl	25
Shut Down Vol. 2	31
CD Bonus Tracks	37
Little Deuce Coupe/All Summer Long	39
Little Deuce Coupe	39
All Summer Long	45
CD Bonus tracks	54
The Beach Boys' Christmas Album	57
Today!/Summer Days... And Summer Nights!	63
The Beach Boys Today!	64
Summer Days... And Summer Nights!	75
CD Bonus tracks	86

Contents

Beach Boys Party!/Stack O' Tracks   89
     Beach Boys Party! 89

Pet Sounds   99

Good Vibrations   119

Smiley Smile/Wild Honey   127
     Smiley Smile 128
     Wild Honey 138
     CD Bonus Tracks 145

Friends/20/20   149
     Friends 149
     20/20 158
     CD Bonus Tracks 168

Beach Boys Concert/Live In London   173
     Beach Boys Concert 173
     Live In London 177
     CD Bonus Tracks 182

References   183

Acknowledgements

This book would not have come into being without the discussions I've had for over half my life with members of the Beach Boys fan community, both online and in person. Most of my knowledge of this band comes not from books - which with a few notable exceptions (listed in the bibliography) are horribly inaccurate - but from these discussions. There's no way I can list all of the people who have contributed in this way, but special thanks should go to Val Johnson-Howe, Ian Alexander-Barnes, Kingsley Abbot, Margaret Dowdle-Head, Iain Harris, Andrew Doe, Tobias Bernsand, blick, topgazza, the late Bob Hanes, Van Dyke Parks, Blake Jones, Paul McNulty, Sean Macreavy, Alex McCambley, Paul Baker, Shawn Taylor, Adam Marsland, Blake Jones, Sean Courtney, Rob McCabe, Annie Wallace, Jon Hunt, John Lane, and more generally all members of the Pet Sounds Mailing List from 1997 through to 2006 and all the regulars at Beach Boys Britain.

The book would also have been very different had I not spent many years making music myself, so I'd like to thank all members of Stealth Munchkin and The National Pep, past and present.

Three resources have been more helpful than any others in checking both the facts and my interpretations of the music. Andrew Doe's Bellagio 10452 site[1] is the definitive

---
[1] http://www.esquarterly.com/bellagio/

word as to the 'plain facts' of the band's career from 1962 through to 1999. Philip Lambert's *Inside The Music Of Brian Wilson* is the best musicological analysis of, specifically, Brian Wilson's music from 1962 through 1967 I've ever read. As you can imagine that book overlaps with this one in a number of areas, and where those overlaps exist Lambert goes into far more detail than I have space for. And finally Francis Greene's transcriptions of the chords for every Beach Boys song[2] have been an absolute Godsend.

Thanks should also go to all those who have encouraged me in my writing in the past, including, but not limited to, Bill Ritchie, Steve Hickey, Lawrence Burton, Simon Bucher-Jones, Andrew Ducker, Andrew Rilstone, Gavin Burrows, Alex Wilcock, Richard Flowers, Mike Taylor, Wesley Osam and Gavin Robinson.

This book was written and typeset in the Free Software text editing program LyX (http://lyx.org), so thanks go to the creators of that software, as well as to the creators of LaTeX, and, ultimately, Donald Knuth, whose typesetting language TeX is the ultimate basis of all those programs. It was created on a machine running the Debian GNU/Linux distribution, so thanks to all the many thousands of people who gave their work freely to that system.

The cover design is courtesy of Mapcase Of Anaheim.

Most importantly, Susan Lang, Tilt Araiza, Christian Lipski, Geoff Howe and Holly Matthies have read through this book in draft form, and made significant corrections, not only of fact and grammar, but also of musical analysis and style.

Where this book is worthwhile and correct, the credit is due them. Where it is dull and incorrect, the blame is mine.

---

[2] http://www.surfermoon.com/tabs.shtml#francis

Introduction

Over this book and its two sequels I'm going to review every available Beach Boys CD, including the solo albums, to try to provide a buyer's guide to the band's music.

The reason for doing this is that I want to have somewhere people can go to get some kind of consistent critical look at the Beach Boys. There are only two books I know of that attempt to analyse the Beach Boys' music in any detail, as opposed to concentrating on a single album or the more lurid aspects of their personal lives, and I would recommend both, but both have their problems. Doe & Tobler's *Complete Guide* is a decent overview for beginners, Andrew Doe is both probably the most knowledgeable person on the band and someone with a good ear for the band's music at its various points, but it's too short and (I believe) out of print. Meanwhile Philip Lambert's *Inside The Music Of Brian Wilson* is one of the best books I've read in many years, and provides a far more in-depth musicological analysis than I would be capable of, but the author has a tendency to remake Brian Wilson in his own image, and the focus is specifically on Brian Wilson (rather than the Beach Boys) and solely on the pre-1967 work.

And this tendency is unfortunate, because the general critical line on the Beach Boys is wrong in two important ways. Firstly, it treats the Beach Boys as being Brian Wilson and a bunch of sidemen. While this was arguably true during the band's commercial heyday (though it's notable that with the exception of the already-famous Jan & Dean, none of Wilson's outside productions troubled the charts at all), the fact is that Mike Love was a better lyricist and bass vocalist than he's given credit for, Carl Wilson and Al Jardine had two of the best voices of the rock era, and Dennis Wilson was a songwriter almost the equal of his big brother.

The other problem is the way it treats Brian Wilson himself. Wilson as a musician is almost an embodiment of the fable about the blind men and the elephant, something that was borne out to me by a terrible article in *Uncut* magazine in 1998, in which the author wanted to prove that Joe Thomas (the producer with whom Wilson was then working) didn't understand Wilson's music and was a bad collaborator. So he asked Wilson's other collaborators, and other musicians. Bruce Johnston, of the Beach Boys, said "Yes, Brian shouldn't be working with Joe Thomas. That's not Brian's real music. He should be making Beach Boys music. Thomas doesn't understand him." Andy Paley, Spector-influenced powerpop songwriter, said "Yes, Brian shouldn't be working with Joe Thomas. That's not Brians real music. He should be making music like Phil Spector and Chuck Berry. Thomas doesn't understand him." and Sean O'Hagan, who makes exotica/lounge-influenced experimental pop, said "Yes, Brian shouldn't be working with Joe Thomas. That's not Brian's real music. He should be making exotica/lounge-influenced experimental pop. Thomas doesn't understand him."

The general critical consensus has another of these partial views of Wilson's work. Everything before *Pet Sounds* was either dreck or classic pop (either way unworthy of analysis). *Pet Sounds* was The Best Album Ever. *Smile* not being finished heralded Brian's Collapse. Everything between *Pet Sounds* and 1974 was rubbish, unless you can apply the word lush, in which case it was A Return To Form. Everything after that was rubbish, unless you can apply the word lush, in which case it was An Unsuccessful Attempt To Trade On Past Glories.

Actually, Wilson's art can't fit into these neat categories. My own take is that the best way to think of Wilson is as an outsider musician, but one who actually happens to have a huge amount of talent. Much like, say, Wesley Willis, Wilson is focused on having huge commercial success, but has little to no idea what actually counts as commercial. He's very easily swayed by people around him, so if he's told he should be doing three-minute pop songs, he does three-minute pop songs, and if he's told he should do epic suites about the American Dream, he does those. But at all times there are two things that remain true about him: he has an unerring ability as an arranger, and a directness that makes his music more communicative than any other music I've ever heard.

But I note that that is only one way of looking at Wilson's music - my way. The last thing I want this book to do is pretend to be definitive.

I'm going to examine, in this book and its two sequels, every Beach Boys studio album, every solo album that's in print (by the classic Mike/ Al/ Carl/ Brian/ Dennis line-up - I've not got the time or inclination to provide thorough reviews of David Marks or Blondie Chaplin's records), and the compilations *Endless Harmony* and *Hawthorne, CA*, and try to explain why the Beach Boys rival the Beatles for musical importance. I'll be doing this by CD, not by album - most Beach Boys albums are currently available as 'twofer' CDs, with two albums and bonus tracks on one CD.

This volume covers all the music the band recorded during their first contract with Capitol Records, from 1962 through 1969, with the exception of the Christmas album, which is now paired on CD with recordings from much later in the band's career. Volume two will cover the band's work from 1970 through to the 1998 death of Carl Wilson, as well as the various archival releases that have been put out since; and volume three will examine the band members' solo albums, from Dennis Wilson's 1977 *Pacific Ocean Blue* to Brian Wilson's 2010 *Brian Wilson Reimagines Gershwin* and Al Jardine's *A Postcard From California* from the same year.

As always, no work is ever finished, only abandoned, and so this may contain mistakes. If you find one, please email me at andrew@thenationalpep.co.uk , and I shall add it to my errata page at http://andrewhickey.info/errata/

But now, let's go surfin'. . .

Surfin' Safari/Surfin' USA

The Beach Boys' first albums were recorded during a time of line-up flux for them. While most bands start recording only after a few years' touring, usually in their early twenties, the Beach Boys were in their teens – rhythm guitarist David Marks being only thirteen. And they had their first hit record, *Surfin'*, before ever having performed live. As a result, it took a while to settle on their 'classic' line-up – while their first single featured that line-up (Brian, Carl and Dennis Wilson, Mike Love and Alan Jardine), the rest of the album, and the next few albums, featured David Marks in place of Jardine. Marks had been part of rehearsals from the start and both Jardine (who returned a year later) and Marks regard each other as 'original' members.

But that it would take a year or so to sort out who was really in the band shows the problem – this is a garage band, quite literally. This is a bunch of teenagers who somehow, accidentally, managed to become huge rock stars at a point where the concept of the rock star was just being formed. What's amazing is that some of this music is competent, or even good, not that most of it's poor.

Surfin' Safari

line-up

Brian Wilson, Carl Wilson, Dennis Wilson, Mike Love, David Marks, Alan Jardine (*Surfin'* only).
  All lead vocals by Mike unless otherwise stated.

Surfin' Safari

The title track of the band's first album is their second single, and first for Capitol Records.
  Essentially a rewrite by Mike and Brian of their earlier single *Surfin'*, it takes all that single's elements and tightens them into a formula that would be repeated in several huge hits for the band (plus *Surf City*, Brian Wilson's number one hit for Jan & Dean) – start with the hook, then have a short verse, mentioning as many different places and pieces of surf slang as possible, sung by Love in his nasal tenor range, followed by a twelve-bar chorus with Love singing a variant of a boogie bassline while the rest of the band chant. Add in a Chuck Berry guitar solo (the only new element in the mix, and a vital one) and fade.
  Other than the brief move to V-of-V in the hook, the only thing of musical interest is the chorus, where the lead vocal takes the bass part, rather than staying on top. Even this early, we're already seeing one of the things that makes Brian Wilson's music different – he writes on the piano, and his left hand is vastly more mobile than his right, playing intricate, complex melodies while his right hand just blocks out chords.
  Later on, when he has five or six voices in the mix, this is what leads to some of his most beautiful vocal parts, but at this point the band were vocally limited – Dave Marks wasn't much of a singer, Dennis was behind the drum kit,

and Carl's voice had barely broken. So we have rudimentary harmonies here, and the lack of more complex vocal parts is what makes this now sound primitive compared to the singles the band would do even a year later.

At this point though, six months before the Beatles even recorded *Love Me Do*, this was a genuinely fresh, interesting sound.

County Fair

Written by Brian and his friend Gary Usher, this story of a date gone wrong features vocal cameos from Andrea Carlo (apparently Dave Marks' aunt, though only 17 at the time) and 'producer' Nik Venet (the A&R man who signed the band to Capitol and took nominal production responsibility for their early recordings) as, respectively, a whining girlfriend and a carnival barker. A rewrite of the Freddie "Boom Boom" Cannon song *Palisades Park* (which the band would much later cover themselves), this was itself later rewritten as *I Do*.

Ten Little Indians

A rewrite by Brian and Gary Usher of the nursery rhyme, this is a two-chord song about little 'Indians' trying to woo a 'squaw' who 'loved the tenth Indian boy'. It features the band singing "kemo sabe" repeatedly and making "wah wah" noises with their hands. In 1962, this was considered acceptable material for a single.

Chug-A-Lug

Another Wilson/Usher song (though Love is also credited, see below), based around the same structure as *Surfin'*

Safari, but this time featuring an organ/guitar solo trade-off. An ode to root beer, the verse lyrics are quick pen portraits of the band and their friends ("Carl says hurry up and order it quick, Dave gets out to chase that chick"). It doesn't really work.

Little Girl (You're My Miss America)

The band's first cover – a song co-written by Herb Alpert, for Dante And His Friends. (The Dante in question was session singer Ron Dante, later better known as the lead vocalist on The Archies' *Sugar Sugar*, and later still Barry Manilow's record producer). A simple Dion-esque ballad, this marks Dennis Wilson's debut as lead vocalist, and he actually does a much better job than anyone else on the record, making this a stand-out track.

409

The B-side of *Surfin' Safari* and written to much the same formula (and, like that track, recorded by the band as a demo before they were signed to Capitol) this is really the start of the Beach Boys we know – far more assured-sounding than anything else on the album (partially thanks to the sound effects recorded in Gary Usher's garage), this shows what the band were capable of when they weren't having to quickly knock out filler.

This was also the start of a run of double-sided singles by the band, where one side would be about surfing (to appeal to the coasts) while the other side would be about cars (to appeal to landlocked middle America) – the car songs tending to be the most popular.

This is one of a number of Beach Boys songs whose authorship is disputed. Until the 1990s it was credited to Brian Wilson and Gary Usher, but in a lawsuit brought by Love this was one of thirty-nine songs for which Love gained co-writer credit.

Some of those songs (for example *California Girls*) were undoubtedly co-written by Love. On others, like *Wouldn't It Be Nice*, one of the other co-writers (in that case lyricist Tony Asher) claimed that Love had no input. In the case of the Usher collaborations, it's hard to know – at the time of the trial, Wilson was mentally unwell, and Gary Usher had died some years earlier. For the record, Love claims in this case to have come up with the 'hooks' "She's real fine, my 409" and "giddy-up 409", with Wilson and Usher writing the rest.

Surfin'

The band's first recording, originally released on tiny indie label Candix, this sounds like the work of a different band, and in many ways it is. At the time this was recorded, the band were still forming, and at this point it sounds like Al Jardine – a folkie and fan of the Kingston Trio – was having a strong influence. The instrumentation is all acoustic – a single acoustic guitar, stand-up bass and one snare drum – and the harmonies are fuller thanks to Jardine's presence. It's little more than a demo, and is a mere sketch of the formula they'd refine on the later early singles. This version is sped up compared to the original recording (the idea of Murry Wilson, the Wilson brothers' father, who was also the band's first manager and another 'producer', to make them sound younger). The original version can be heard on the *Good Vibrations* box set.

Heads You Win, Tails I Lose

A fairly nondescript Wilson/Usher track, notable mostly for managing to make the line "Why can't we arbitrarily resolve a fight?" work in context.

Summertime Blues

A cover of the Eddie Cochrane song, with lead vocals sung as a unison duet by Carl Wilson and David Marks, this sounds exactly like you'd expect a fourteen- and a fifteen-year-old singing this song in unison to sound. Mike Love injects some wit and panache when he takes the low "No dice, son" parts.

Cuckoo Clock

An utterly undistinguished Wilson/Usher track, notable only for being Brian Wilson's first lead vocal to be released.

Moon Dawg

A cover of a track by The Gamblers. The original is interesting for several reasons, as it features both Bruce Johnston (later himself a member of the Beach Boys) and Elliot "Winged Eel Fingerling" Ingber (later of the Mothers Of Invention and Captain Beefheart's Magic Band) as well as having, on its B-side, the very first song ever to reference LSD (*LSD-25* – in 1962, remember!). The original was also produced by Nik Venet, who is credited on early pressings of the Beach Boys' record (but not the original Gamblers track) as the composer (later pressings credit Derry Weaver, the Gamblers' guitarist). Unfortunately, it's a generic surf instrumental, and the Beach Boys' version is a rather amateurishly-played generic surf instrumental.

The Shift

The band's first exercise in sexism finishes the album up. Apparently if you "get your girl a shift and she'll look real fine" and "[a girl] wearing a shift really turns me on". They repeat how much this particular one-piece bathing suit "turns [them] on" in case we didn't realise. Mike Love wrote the lyrics, unsurprisingly.

Surfin' USA

line-up

Brian Wilson, Carl Wilson, Dennis Wilson, Mike Love, David Marks.

Surfin' USA

Rather surprisingly, at least for non-fans, this was the last uptempo surf-themed hit single the band recorded (not counting 1968′s nostalgia track *Do It Again*) – while Brian Wilson would keep hammering away at his formula with Jan & Dean for a couple of years (*Surf City*, *Ride The Wild Surf* etc), this track is it, as far as the Beach Boys' uptempo surf hits go. They'd have one more surf-themed song, the ballad *Surfer Girl*, and that would be it.

This is also the first Beach Boys track to feature Brian Wilson's falsetto being given a quick solo spot, something that would become an increasingly prominent part of the band's sound, though Love takes the lead apart from that one line.

While this was the work of many hands, including Wilson, probably Love, and Wilson's girlfriend's brother (who provided the place-names), Wilson was credited as sole songwriter originally. But then Chuck Berry sued, on the not-unreasonable grounds that the whole melody and arrangement (right down to the stop-start guitar) was stolen from *Sweet Little Sixteen*, so Berry is now credited as sole author.

Farmer's Daughter

A Wilson/Love song with Brian Wilson taking a solo falsetto lead. A mildly smutty (for the time) song from the point of view of a traveller who stops off for a couple of days and 'help[s] you plough your fields'. Hem hem. For some unknown reason, Fleetwood Mac (the *Rumours* version) used to cover this live.

Misirlou

The first of five (count 'em!) surf instrumentals on the album, this is a very careful, reverent cover of Dick Dale's version of this old instrumental. One can practically hear Carl Wilson sticking his tongue out in concentration as he plays the difficult bits.

Stoked

This instrumental is credited as written by Brian Wilson. That's assuming anything quite so rudimentary ever needed 'writing'.

The Lonely Sea

A Wilson/Usher ballad that anticipates much of Wilson's later work, being a bridge between *Surfer Girl* (written but not released until the next album) and *In My Room*, with its slow guitar arpeggios and falsetto lead. The words are utterly rudimentary, and there's a bathetic brief spoken section ("this pain in my heart/these tears in my eyes/please tell the truth"), but somehow it still manages to have an incredibly haunting effect.

One piece of advice though – don't listen to the stereo mix with headphones. The lead vocal and all instruments are in one channel, and the backing vocals isolated in the other. Which would be fine, except the backing vocals only come in half-way through, but the mic was open the entire time, picking up coughs, salival noises and breaths. If Mike Love heavy-breathing in your ear for 90 seconds sounds like fun, go ahead, but otherwise stick to speakers...

Shut Down

The B-side to *Surfin' USA*, this shows the Chuck Berry influence in a different way. Where the A-side had just stolen one of Berry's melodies, this one has its own melody (a development on from that of *409*) but the words are an attempt to write a Chuck Berry car-race song in the style of *Maybelline* or *You Can't Catch Me*.

That they work that well is thanks to the lyricist, the DJ Roger Christian, who Brian Wilson had heard critiquing the lyrics to *409* on the radio and who became a frequent collaborator with Wilson, Jan Berry and Gary Usher (together and separately) for the next few years.

Christian's car-song lyrics (and Love's car songs, when he's imitating Christian) were more sophisticated than the surf lyrics had been, frequently having a plot with some kind of conflict and resolution. While this is based on *409*, we can see clear traces of this song in *Little Deuce Coupe* (similar melody), *I Get Around* ("round, round get around, I get around" and "tach it up, tach it up, buddy gonna shut you down" having similar functions in the songs) and *Fun, Fun, Fun* (the backing vocals acting as a Greek chorus in the second verse), among others – this was a big step forward for Wilson.

While it's not perfect – Love's lead vocal is horribly double-tracked in the last verse – it's charming enough that things like Love's two-note sax honking 'solo' sound endearing rather than amateurish, and it's a great little single. This is another song over whose credits Love sued and won in the 1990s.

Noble Surfer

Because, you see, "noble" sounds a tiny bit like "no bull", which if you're in 1962 is a tiny bit rude. This astounding realisation which changed the course of humour forever was hit on by Mike Love, and Brian Wilson set the mirthtastic laugh-riot to music that fits it perfectly.

Honky Tonk

Bill Doggett's original of this (with guitarist Billy Butler) is a rock & roll classic, one of the great R&B instrumentals of all time, slow, dark and grooving over two sides of a 45. This is two minutes and four seconds of teenagers playing with too much echo. By this point Carl Wilson was a very competent teenage guitarist, but this is still absolutely pointless.

Lana

A rewrite of *Farmer's Daughter* with a little of *The Shift* thrown in, musically. Lyrically, though, it's a bland love song. Brian Wilson takes both lead vocal and solo composition credit.

Surf Jam

Ostensibly written by Carl Wilson. Which is odd, because the only Wilson on the credits for *Wipe Out* by the Surfaris is Ron Wilson.

Let's Go Trippin'

A cover of a Dick Dale track that is distinguished from every other generic surf instrumental ever by the truly strange reverb effect on Dale's guitar. Guess which feature of the track they didn't copy? They did add the sax 'talents' of Mike Love though...

Finders Keepers

This rounds out the biggest load of tossed-together nothing the band would release in the first twenty-five years of their career with a rewrite of *Heads You Win, Tails I Lose* from the previous album, but done slightly more interestingly. Not much more, though. A Brian and Mike track.

CD Bonus Tracks

Cindy, Oh Cindy

A cover of a nondescript fifties pop ballad about going to sea and missing one's girl. Brian turns in a decent vocal performance, and while this is far from exciting it's much better than half of what was on the *Surfin' USA* album, and should probably have been released rather than left in the can.

The Baker Man

Another unreleased song, which sounds like an attempt to rewrite *Hully Gully* as a girl-group dance song in the style of *The Locomotion*. Brian turns in a surprisingly good gruff vocal, but the song itself is fluff and overlong. That said, it's still better than half of *Surfin' USA*.

Land Ahoy

A Brian Wilson song in a similar style to *Cindy, Oh Cindy*, another song of sailors pining for their love. It was rerecorded a few months later as *Cherry, Cherry Coupe* but neither track is hugely successful. Mike Love sings lead.

Surfer Girl/Shut Down Vol. 2

It shows how fast the pop music industry moved in the early 1960s that the Beach Boys released their third and fourth albums in the same month, September 1963, less than a year after their first. *Little Deuce Coupe*, their fourth album, suffered as a result – a concept album of sorts, based on car songs, it shared two songs with *Surfer Girl* and also took one each from the previous two albums, as the band simply couldn't come up with material fast enough.

This means that the CD 'twofer' pairings have a slight chronological inaccuracy – the two September 1963 albums, rather than being paired with each other, are each paired with a 1964 record, thus avoiding repetition of tracks. As I'm dealing with these records on a per-CD basis, that's how I'll be looking at them too.

Surfer Girl

The pressure to produce new music at an incredible pace had made Brian Wilson want to give up touring and concentrate on writing and production. As a result, Al Jardine, who had sung and played bass on the band's first single, was drafted in to replace him on the road and augment the band in the studio. This line-up wouldn't last long, however, as shortly after the release of this album David Marks fell out with Murry Wilson, the band's manager and father of the Wilson brothers (and Mike Love's uncle), and was either sacked from or quit the band, leaving Jardine as his replacement and Brian Wilson back on tour for the moment.

Jardine's return saw the band's style finally gel – adding a strong tenor vocal part to the mid-range of the band's harmony stack finally allowed the band to be the vocal group Brian Wilson had always intended them to be – from this point on the four- and five-part harmonies start to resemble less the simplistic records of Jan & Dean and more the sophisticated jazz harmonies of Brian's teen idols the Four Freshmen.

line-up

Brian Wilson, Carl Wilson, Dennis Wilson, Mike Love, David Marks, Al Jardine (uncredited)

Surfer Girl

Supposedly the first song Brian Wilson ever wrote (though presumably the lyrics were only added after the band started writing surf songs), this song had been demoed at the same sessions that produced *Surfin' Safari* and *409*, and it remains a mystery why this was left off the earlier albums when so many terrible songs were included. A rewrite of *When You Wish Upon A Star*, with the same arpeggiated guitar feel as *The Lonely Sea*, this is the first real harmony work-out for the band, sung as a close harmony number with Brian's falsetto soaring across the top.

SURFER GIRL

It's not a perfect performance – the middle-eight double-tracking is slightly sloppy – but it's far more assured than anything they'd done previously. It's also the most harmonically interesting thing the band had done to date. While it's mostly just a I-vi-IV-V7 doo-wop progression, it does have a minor sixth (v6) at the end of every other line ('undone' and 'ocean's roar') which anticipates the later use of minor sixths in songs like *God Only Knows*.

It's also the first of the Beach Boys' records to feature a key change (unless I missed one on the first two albums, but I don't think so) – having a semitone step up for the last verse. Released as a single, this became the band's last surf-related single to be released during their American chart peak, as well as the first to be credited to Brian Wilson as producer.

Catch A Wave

Comparing this song to any on the previous two albums shows just how far the band had come in production terms. Harmonically simple, this insanely catchy track is nonetheless a far more sophisticated record than anything they'd done before, with a piano doubling the two guitars in an early example of a technique Brian had learned from Phil Spector, an overdubbed *Palisades Park* organ riff, harp glissandi (provided by Mike Love's sister Maureen), and a traded-off organ/guitar solo that presages the similar solo used in *Fun, Fun, Fun*. This would have been a stand-out track on the earlier albums, but here it's just another track. A Brian Wilson/Mike Love song, Love's lyrics would later be replaced by Roger Christian and turned into *Sidewalk Surfin'*, a minor hit for Jan & Dean.

The Surfer Moon

The second Brian Wilson solo composition of the album is an unsuccessful rewrite of the first. The verse chord sequence is almost a clone of that of *Surfer Girl*, right down to the minor sixth, although the middle eight is surprisingly sophisticated. It's let down though by the lyrics, which literally resort to moon/June rhymes, and the string arrangement (the first on a Beach Boys record) which apes the muzaky sound of the Four Freshmen and other 50s easy-listening acts. A solo vocal performance by Brian, this is still far ahead of anything from the first two albums, and points forward to the romanticism of later works like *Today!* and *Pet Sounds*, but doesn't really work.

South Bay Surfer

Credited to Brian and Carl Wilson and Al Jardine, this is a rewrite of the old Stephen Foster song *Old Folks At Home*, which must have been on Brian Wilson's mind at the time, as he also recorded a track with his wife's band, the Honeys, based on the same tune (*Surfin' Down The Swanee River*). Nothing special, this is mostly notable as being the first song where Al Jardine is really noticeable in the vocals, singing the top line of the harmonies (such as they are, being mostly Brian, Carl and Al chanting in near-unison).

The Rocking Surfer

One of the last of the surf-style instrumentals the band did, this alternates a simple Hammond organ statement of a rather dull melody - the melody used by the Good Humor ice cream trucks of the time - with some relatively competent guitar work. The whole thing's drowned in hiss too, due presumably to poor quality tape. Another Brian Wilson solo credit, this at least has the decency to be credited trad. arr, as presumably nobody could believe this actually needed to be written.

Little Deuce Coupe

The B-side to *Surfer Girl*, this charted separately itself at number 15 in the US. Written by Brian Wilson and Roger Christian, this is one of the songs Mike Love sued over, and if you compare the lyrics on the demo (on the *Hawthorne, CA* rarities CD) you can see that there were certainly alterations made before the recording. Recorded at the last session before Al rejoined the band (and the first where Brian was credited as official producer), this track shows the band's influence shifting from Chuck Berry to more groove-based shuffle music like Fats Domino.

To the ears of an Englishman (and one, furthermore, who can't drive) the lyrics are utter gibberish, but I am reliably informed that "She's got a competition clutch with four on the floor and she purrs like a kitten til the lake pipes roar/and if that ain't enough to make you flip your lid, there's one more thing I got the pink slip daddy" is in fact in English... One of the best of the band's early hits.

In My Room

This is one of the most beautiful songs ever written, by Gary Usher and Brian Wilson. A refinement of the *Surfer Girl* formula, and like that based on arpeggiated triplets following something akin to the standard doo-wop changes (though extended and altered) with block harmonies, this is one of the times when utter simplicity is the most effective musical and lyrical technique.

A song about both comfort and loneliness, this track is much more ambiguous than it might seem, being about both Brian Wilson's escaping from his abusive father by hiding away in the music room and about sharing his bedroom with his brothers (the first two voices we hear after Brian's) growing up and harmonising with them as they sang themselves to sleep, but Gary Usher's simple lyric manages to take these experiences and universalise them. Featuring all six Beach Boys plus Maureen Love on harp, this is the stand-out track of the band's first four albums, and if they'd never recorded anything else this track would still have been enough to make the Beach Boys' reputation.

Hawaii

Recorded the same day as *Catch A Wave*, much like that song Mike Love's vocals show evidence of a sore throat, and he sounds spookily like his cousin Dennis for much of the song. A great little pop song by Brian and Mike that can never quite decide whether it's in C, D or G, this is a standout track that could easily have been a hit single and remains in the touring 'Beach Boys' repertoire to this day.

Surfers Rule

A filler track about how 'surfers' are better than 'hodaddies', written by Brian and Mike with a rudimentary lead vocal by Dennis. It's mostly notable for the fadeout, where the song turns into a challenge against the band's East Coast rivals the Four Seasons, with the band singing "Surfers rule (Four Seasons, you'd better believe it)" while Brian imitates Frankie Valli's *Walk Like A Man* falsetto over the top.

Our Car Club

A not-especially-good Wilson/Love song turned into a rather interesting production, all low Duane Eddy throbbing guitar and sax and pulsating drums. The young-sounding falsetto vocals don't really work well with the backing track, but it's an interesting experiment. And again, I might appreciate the song more if I had any idea what lines like "We'll really cut some low ETs" meant. Or maybe not.

Your Summer Dream

A more effective attempt at *The Surfer Moon*, a solo Brian vocal over lush chords (almost all minor 7ths). While not one of the best songs on the album, this is much better than the earlier track, as not only is the chord sequence slightly more original, with a nice melancholy tinge to it, but Bob Norberg's lyrics are far better than anything Brian Wilson could come up with on his own.

And to finish an album that, while still patchy, is exponentially better than either of the first two, is the generic instrumental

Boogie Woodie

Credited to Rimsky-Korsakov arr. Brian Wilson, this is supposedly based around *Flight of the Bumble-bee*, but sounds far more like *Pinetop's Boogie Woogie* to my ears.

Shut Down Vol. 2

The band's first album of 1964 was also the first by what is now regarded as the 'classic' five-man line-up of the band (which would stay in this formation for not much more than a year). A mixed bag, this album more than any other shows how bands still weren't thinking in terms of albums – the best material on here is as good as the best music recorded by anyone ever, and the worst is so bad as to be laughable. The album's title is a subtle dig at Capitol records, the band's label, who had put out a cash-in compilation called Shut Down, featuring a couple of Beach Boys tracks alongside people such as Robert Mitchum.

line-up

Brian Wilson, Carl Wilson, Dennis Wilson, Mike Love, Al Jardine.

Fun, Fun, Fun

One of the most exciting of the band's early hits, this song was almost begging for another lawsuit from Chuck Berry, having an intro that is note-for-note identical to that of *Johnny B Goode*. Rather amazingly the lawsuit never came. (I've also heard it claimed that the verse melody was taken from Berry's *Carol*, but I can hear very little resemblance).

Based on a true story (which happened either to a girlfriend of Dennis Wilson or the daughter of a DJ in Utah, depending on whose story you believe), this is one of several songs on this album whose creation is the subject of wildly differing accounts – Mike Love claims it was written in a cab in Salt Lake City, while Brian Wilson says they wrote it in Australia, after seeing the Beatles on TV.

Either way, the competition from the Beatles (who had not yet had a hit in the US when the song was recorded, but who were known to the band by this point after their Australian tour) clearly motivated the band to up their game, and everything about this track is exceptional, from Mike

Love's lyric (one of his very best) to the backing vocals acting as a Greek chorus, to the duelling Hammond and guitar solo, to Brian's falsetto soaring over everything as the track fades. The single mix (included as a bonus track on the CD) is the superior one, but this is a wonderful track in either form.

Don't Worry Baby

The second track on the album is even better. Based loosely on the Ronettes' *Be My Baby* which Brian Wilson considers the greatest single ever recorded, with a little of *Walking In The Rain* for good measure, this changes that adolescent sexual longing for something altogether more personal.

We see time and again in Brian Wilson's music the figure of the woman who can save a man who is let down by his own weaknesses, and this is in fact the key to pretty much everything Wilson did (and one reason why although people compare him to Paul McCartney he is far closer to John Lennon, the only other songwriter in popular music to be as obsessed with masculine weakness being saved by a strong woman). This is the first time this figure appears, and it's probably no coincidence that this song was written around the time of two pivotal events in Wilson's life – his first nervous breakdown (on the 'plane on the way to an Australian tour) and his engagement to his first wife, Marilyn.

Roger Christian puts this vulnerability and need for help into a typical Beach Boys context – someone afraid to drive in a drag race, but unable to back out because of his own bragging – but what really matters is just that this is a man trapped in a traditional masculine role, and only the unnamed 'she' can help him escape, when she says "Don't worry baby, everything will turn out all right"

Musically, as well, this is very typically Brian Wilson. I've talked before about how he's very much a piano-based composer and chords out with his right hand while playing melodies with his left, and this can be seen here better than anywhere else. On the chorus, Mike Love is clearly singing the moving left hand piano part ("Now don't/now don't you wo/rry ba-by"), the rest of the band are singing the block right-hand chords ("Don't worry baby/Don't worry ba-by"), while Brian is singing the melody line he would have been singing while playing the piano, on top ("Don't worry baby/everything will turn out all right/Don't worry baby").

This is just a stunning, beautiful song and performance, and when released as the B-side to *I Get Around* managed to chart at number 24 in the US in its own right. In fact MOJO magazine, in the late 1990s, did a 'hundred greatest singles of all time' list and this came in at number 15, despite being a B-side.

In The Parkin' Lot

Another Wilson/Christian song, this is filler about which there is essentially nothing to say, except that the intro and outro have nice harmonies.

"Cassius" Love vs "Sunny" Wilson

Even less essential, being a 'comedy' spoken-word section where the band pretend to be rehearsing for a show, with bits of their hit records interspersed with Mike and Brian making fun of each others' voices.

The Warmth Of The Sun

This, however, gets us back to *Don't Worry Baby* levels of quality. Written by Brian and Mike either the night before or the night after the JFK assassination, depending on who you believe, this is the most sophisticated, complex version of the *Surfer Girl* formula the band ever did.

It sounds at first like a simple rewrite of that song, being another 12/8 arpeggiated track with block harmonies, starting out with the familiar doo-wop changes, but those changes soon go in a radically different direction. The I-vi-ii-V (or the variant I-vi-IV-V) chord progression (doo-wop changes or 'four chord trick') is the basis of literally tens of thousands of songs, from *Blue Moon* and *Heart And Soul* to *Please Mister Postman*, *This Boy* and *I Will Always Love You*. And this song's first two chords, C and Am, follow that pattern precisely. But then rather than go to the expected Dm, the song changes key to E♭ (a tone-and-a-half up), restarts the progression, and continues that until it gets to Dm, where it stays twice as long as it 'should' before finishing the original progression in C, so we have I-vi-III♭-i-ii-ii-V-Vaug (the Beatles did something similar to this in *Day Tripper*, but using a 12-bar blues rather than doo-wop changes).

As well as being musically clever, though, this also suits the mood of the song – the song is about loss, and hope after loss, and by moving from C through to Cm back to C again, that feeling of loss followed by renewed hope is conveyed in the chords – musically it's like going through the night and getting to the dawn again. *Warmth Of The Sun* is one of those songs that by rights should be a standard, one of the most perfect songs ever written.

This Car Of Mine

A Dion-esque song by Mike and Brian, written to give Dennis a vocal spot. It's catchy enough, but has nothing of any real interest about it.

Why Do Fools Fall In Love?

A fairly straight cover of the Frankie Lymon & The Teenagers classic from the fifties, with a nice added *a capella* statement of the title in the middle of the song. One of the band's best covers, but not hugely different from the original.

Pom Pom Play Girl

Carl Wilson's first solo lead vocal, on a Wilson/Usher song that has little to recommend it – musically it's a rewrite of *Little Deuce Coupe* while lyrically it's a rather nastily misogynist portrait of a cheerleader who "doesn't really know why she's waving her hands".

Keep An Eye On Summer

Another 12/8 doo-wop based song, written by Brian Wilson and Bob Norberg (with Love gaining credit in his lawsuit). Bearing a slight resemblance to the Four Freshmen's *Graduation Day*, which was in the band's live repertoire at the time, this is nothing special. Strangely, this was one of two Beach Boys songs Brian chose to rerecord for his 1998 solo album *Imagination*.

Shut Down Part II

Another generic surf instrumental, credited to Carl Wilson but again the kind of thing any band knock outs in a jam session. It starts with Mike Love reprising his two-note sax 'solo' from *Shut Down*, presumably to justify the title.

Louie Louie

A pretty poor cover, with Carl Wilson actually enunciating the lyrics, although Love's dumb 'duh-duh-duh' bass vocal has just the right kind of stupidity (sounding very like some of the backing vocals on early Zappa records).

Denny's Drums

A solo drum performance, supposedly by Dennis Wilson, who is credited as composer, but suspicious minds might think it was actually session player Hal Blaine...

CD Bonus Tracks

Fun, Fun, Fun (single mix)

This is a slightly different mix to the album mix, with Brian's vocal higher in the mix on the fade, and a drum overdub, but little other difference.

Ganz Allein

In My Room sung in German, to the same backing track.

I Do

A Brian Wilson song that was eventually given to The Castells, a harmony-pop band whose lead singer later joined the Gary Usher-produced Hondells. Recorded around the time of the *Surfer Girl* sessions, this sounds like it was influenced by some of Phil Spector's work with the Crystals, and would have made a better album track than many of the filler tracks that did get released.

Little Deuce Coupe/All Summer Long

The Beach Boys' fourth album, *Little Deuce Coupe*, came out three weeks after their third, *Surfer Girl*. A concept album of sorts, based around cars, it included four songs from earlier albums. This means that the CD 'twofer' pairings have a slight chronological inaccuracy – the two September 1963 albums, rather than being paired with each other, are each paired with a 1964 record, thus avoiding repetition of tracks. As I'm dealing with these records on a per-CD basis, that's how I'll be looking at them too.

Little Deuce Coupe

The last album to feature David Marks, before his disagreements with the Wilsons' father Murry led him to leave to form his own band, The Marksmen, this album nonetheless has the stronger harmonies that show that Al Jardine was firmly in place. A collection of car songs, it's clearly a rush job, but it still has its moments. It is, though, far from essential – it was recorded in a single session, and sounds it.

line-up

Brian Wilson, Carl Wilson, Dennis Wilson, Mike Love, David Marks, Al Jardine (uncredited)

Little Deuce Coupe

The same recording included on the *Surfer Girl* album

Ballad Of Ole' Betsy

Another rewrite of *The Surfer Moon/Your Summer Dream* from the previous album, this is the best of these three attempts at what amounts to the same musical material, thanks to being the only one to feature full band vocals. This brings out the Four Freshmen influence more obviously, and other than a double tracking error on 'she may be rusted iron' the vocals are gorgeous, especially on the *a capella* tag.

The lyrics, by Roger Christian, are less impressive, anthropomorphising a car – "she was born in '32, and was she ever pretty/she rode a freight train west, all the way from Detroit city" and so on. This manages to make them both over-sentimental mush about what is, after all, an inanimate object, while simultaneously seeming to objectify women in a rather disturbing way ("Betsy took some beatings, but she never once complained"...) But if you listen for the vocals, and ignore both text and subtext, it works as a piece of music.

Be True To Your School

A musically uninteresting piece of boosterism by Love and Brian Wilson, bearing some slight musical resemblance

LITTLE DEUCE COUPE   41

to *Hawaii* (whose tag is reused at the end). I'm not the target audience for this track as I never had the American High School experience, and I've always loathed both sports and expressions of in-group solidarity (especially when they're expressed in an aggressive manner – "we'll be ready to fight, we're gonna smash 'em now"). If you're the kind of person who likes that kind of thing, you might have a less jaded impression of this track.

Car Crazy Cutie

A reworking of a doo-wop track Brian had written for another band, The Survivors, a short while earlier, with new lyrics by Roger Christian about a beautiful girlfriend who is more interested in cars than the singer – "But when I talk of lovin' man, some kisses and hugs/She says don't you think we'd better clean and gap the plugs".

This is actually something of a theme on this album – the disconnect between appearance and actuality. Along with the fact that so much of the musical material is reused (either from rejected earlier songs, songs given to other people, or just sticking an old record on the album to fill up the gaps), there are some quite interesting collisions of form and content going on here. The album is about taking old junk and polishing it up to make it look good, but it still being less than perfect under the hood.

The fact that they take the same attitude towards women as to cars and their songs is unfortunate, but probably to be expected given their ages (the band members ranged from fifteen to twenty-two) and the culture they were in.

The lack of success with this 'cutie' though is probably why Brian is the lead vocalist, as otherwise this Dion pastiche would have been a perfect vocal showcase for Dennis. But his swaggering persona would never have worked with the rejection in the last verse. This is still, however, by far the best new song on the album.

Cherry, Cherry Coupe

A rewrite of the then-unreleased *Land Ahoy* by Brian and Roger Christian, which appears to be about a particularly good car. I say 'appears to be' because here we run into one of the problems in reviewing this album for a British person born in 1978 who doesn't drive, is that a good chunk of the lyrics don't seem to be in anything I'd recognise as English. I haven't a clue what "My coupe's tuck and roll underneath the hood" or "Chrome reversed rims with whitewall slicks" are. Are they a good thing? "Chopped nose and deck with louvers on the hood" ? I take it these are good things, because "It's the sharpest in the town and the envy of my group", but for all I know this could be advocating the violent overthrow of the government and its replacement with a fascist dictatorship.

That might be what a cellunoid system is. . .

That said, this is catchy enough, and one of the first times Mike Love is allowed to really impress with his bass range – his tenor lead here is merely passable, but on the choruses his bass rumbling of "My cherry coupe eats 'em up coming off the line/And she really gets lost when she starts to whine" makes the song.

409

The track from the *Surfin' Safari* album

Shut Down

The track from the *Surfin' USA* album

Spirit Of America

It shows how desperate the Beach Boys were getting for material that this and *Ballad Of Ole Betsy* were included on the same album, despite having near-identical melodies. This Wilson/Christian song, with Brian Wilson on lead vocal, is about Craig Breedlove's first world land speed record, which he had achieved four weeks to the day before the recording session for this album.

Given the circumstances one wouldn't expect a masterpiece, and the fact that the track is even competent says a lot for how good Brian Wilson was at this point. It seems at times like I'm slating this album – and it really isn't very good by any normal standards – but to record something this adequate in the time they were given is frankly astounding.

Our Car Club

The same recording included on the *Surfer Girl* album

No-Go Showboat

I think this is an attempt at a comedy song – I say I think, because again this is a Roger Christian lyric, which means the lyrics are full of things like "It really rates fine in the custom clan, with hand-formed panels, tuck-and-roll rear pan". But I *think* it's about a car which looks good but won't go fast ("When it comes to speed, man, I'm just outa luck, I'm even shut down by the ice cream truck").

A Young Man Is Gone

Bobby Troup's maudlin *Their Hearts Were Full Of Spring*, a song recorded by the Four Freshmen, was one of the first things the Beach Boys ever recorded, and has remained in the band's act to this day as an *a capella* showcase.

It's fascinating if you have access to enough live recordings to hear how the different voices entering and leaving the line-up over the years have affected the quality of the harmonies – to my mind the best version is the rehearsal recording from 1993 with only two original members of the band (Carl and Al) plus Bruce Johnston and Al's son Matt.

This is their only official studio recording of the song, with new lyrics by Mike Love, here bemoaning the death of James Dean, and while the original lyrics were bad, these are, if anything, worse:

> For this daring young star met his death while in his car
>
> No one knows the reason why
>
> Screaming tyre, flashing fire, and gone was this young star
>
> Oh how could they let him die

However, the harmonies are exquisite, and the whole thing just about works because of that.

Custom Machine

The last song on this album is also by far the most interesting, although it falls into the category of 'interesting failure' – *Custom Machine* has quite a lot of playing around with keys and tonality, with the chorus seeming to go off into some nowhere between-keys land (on the line "I'll let you look but don't touch my custom machine").

However, it sounds arbitrary, rather than clever – an experiment that didn't quite come off.

The track still almost works, mostly down to the band's enthusiasm and tightness – a tightness that's even more surprising when you realise how little time they (and the session musicians augmenting them) had to rehearse and learn the song – you can hear someone whispering the next line to Mike Love during the instrumental break.

Originally credited as a solo Brian Wilson composition, this is one of the songs for which Mike Love won a co-writing credit in his 1990s lawsuit. To my ears, though, it sounds if anything like a Roger Christian lyric – Love's lyrics usually have the virtue of being singable and in something approaching English, while lines like "A stereophonic speaker set with vibrasonic sound" just sit uncomfortably, having far too many syllables for their melody.

All Summer Long

While *Shut Down Vol 2* had contained two of the best tracks the band would ever record, plus one of their biggest hits, *All Summer Long* is the point where the Beach Boys, spurred on by at last having some real competition, became important. This was the start of their four-album golden period (this, *Today!*, *Summer Days... And Summer Nights!* and *Pet Sounds*) where they were not only having huge hits but making huge artistic strides forward as well.

I once played a Beatles album for a relative who didn't really know their work, and he said to me half-way through "No, I want to hear a proper album, not a collection of hits" – *All Summer Long*, more than any other Beach Boys album, feels like that. While only one track became an actual hit single, four of its eleven tracks were included on the *Endless Summer* compilation and pretty much every hits compilation and best-of since, while another, *Little Honda*, became a huge hit in a note-for-note cover version by the Hondells.

While it still has its share of filler (the Beach Boys never really became an 'album band' until they were almost commercially obsolete), this is the earliest Beach Boys album about which one can say it's an essential album, rather than just having essential tracks.

line-up

Brian Wilson, Carl Wilson, Dennis Wilson, Mike Love, Al Jardine

I Get Around

You may have heard this one...

The Beach Boys' first number one, this is the first of their singles to show signs of having been constructed as a record first and song second. If Mike Love (who won co-writing credit for this in 1993, before which it was credited as a Brian Wilson solo composition) is telling the truth, in fact, when he claims to have come up with the "round, round, get around" hook, then he can probably lay claim to 90% of the record's success.

But that other 10% is crucial, and is all down to the structure and production, which is stunningly sophisticated. First just listen to the way the instrumental track is carefully layered. We start with two low notes on the guitar – but then there is no instrumentation for the next four seconds. Going into the chorus, we can hear a guitar and bass (a fairly poor lead guitar part was recorded but is not audible in the final mix), both essentially doubling each other (a trick Brian had learned from Phil Spector), and a very interesting drum part courtesy of Dennis Wilson (the basic track) and session player Hal Blaine (overdubs).

With almost no hi-hat or cymbal at all, the part on the record consists of just a kick drum every other beat and one fill two bars in, along with some incredibly fast brushwork. Rather amazingly, this brushwork is the replacement for a harpsichord part – if one listens to the session recordings (not that I would ever advocate illegal downloading of course hem hem), the same part, in more or less the same range, is being played by the harpsichord (Blaine is playing semiquavers, while the harpsichord was playing quavers, but the audible pressing and release of the keys doubled it rhythmically). In fact the drum part seems to be a construction after the fact rather than a live performance – the basic track for the song, before any overdubbing, features a far more conventional drum pattern, with fours on the kick drum, snare for emphasis every other beat (where the kick drum is on the record) and quavers on the hi-hat.

It's only after the basic track is done that the drums are re-recorded (although one can still very faintly hear leakage from the original hi-hat track used to keep time through the *a capella* sections).

We then have the verse, where while Mike Love's singing we have two bars of just guitar and bass doubling each other in a stop-start rhythm (with a stray hi-hat beat to keep them in time) under the first line, before being joined by handclaps for the second line, before a two-bar instrumental break. This break does feature the harpsichord, but it's overwhelmed by the hammond organ that's added.

This two-bar break (stretching the verse to an unusual ten bar length) contains musical material found nowhere else, but which Terry Melcher (of whom much more, sadly, in volume two) would re-use as the main guitar riff for the Byrds' version of *Mister Tambourine Man* (the backing track of which was based on this song's B-side, *Don't Worry Baby*). We then go into a repeat of the chorus, instrumentally the same as the intro, which goes into a new, short section, the 'get around round round ooh' section, and again we can feel the tension building as through these rising oohs we add in the hammond organ, a lead guitar solo and, barely audible, three bass saxophone notes at crucial points.

We've gone from a single voice and practically no instrumentation right up to a full wall of sound, and it's been a natural progression, like a driver slowly pressing his foot down and taking you from 0 to 100 without ever really noticing the acceleration. And the instrumental track isn't even what we notice on this track, it's those five part harmonies, and Brian Wilson's falsetto soaring like it never had before. It's the sense of restlessness coupled with braggadocio – of someone who knows he's absolutely mastered the pop single, and is itching to try something better ("I'm getting bugged driving up and down the same old strip, I gotta find a new place where the kids are hip").

Were it not that that accolade truly belongs to a single the Beach Boys would release two years later, one could easily describe *I Get Around* as the perfect pop record.

All Summer Long

Anything was going to be a let-down after that opener, but truth be told I've never been a huge fan of this song even divorced from its context. While it's interesting from a production standpoint (the xylophone part was an inspired move) and harmonically (it's essentially a variant on the I-vi-ii-V progression, but replacing the minor sixth with a flattened third, a rather jazzy substitution, and then extending a lot of the chords with passing sixths and augmented fifths). While this song's use in *American Graffitti* kick-started the band's commercial revival in the mid-70s, I have to say I've always found it too saccharine. And, though it's hardly fair to judge it on this, the trade-off between the whistle and saxophone on the instrumental break can't help but make any British people with a love of comedy think that someone's playing a game of Swanee Kazoo. This is another song for which Mike Love, who sings lead, sued and won co-writing credit.

Hushabye

The only actual cover on the album (though see *Carl's Big Chance*) this is a fairly straight cover of a doo-wop song, originally recorded by the Mystics.

Written by the great songwriting team of Doc Pomus and Mort Shuman (responsible for roughly seventeen trillion quadrillion of the great pop songs of the late 50s and early 60s) they were having a comparative off-day when they came up with this – other than the melodic referencing of Brahms' *Lullaby* in the middle eight, this is a fairly standard doo-wop song. The performance and production here is absolutely exemplary – the harmonies are heavenly, the broken drum part and driving piano bass are the missing link between what Phil Spector was doing at the time and what the Beatles would be doing by the end of the year – but this is 'only' a very, very pleasant trifle. Brian sings lead, with Mike on the middle eight.

Little Honda

A Wilson/Love song for which there's never been any credit dispute, this is one of those songs where you can see what an influence the band had on the Velvet Underground.

From the throbbing low-range three-chord guitar to the held organ notes (a common thing in Brian Wilson's arrangements, often filling in what would be another harmony part in the middle of the stack), to the monotone lead vocal melody, this is musically extremely close to songs like *Foggy Notion*, *White Light/White Heat* or *I'm Waiting For The Man*. There's even a drone, courtesy of the hummed backing vocals in the verse. Of course, the Velvet Underground rarely had lyrics like "It's more fun than a barrel of monkeys, that two-wheel bike", but frankly that's the Velvets' problem, not the Beach Boys'.

We'll Run Away

A weak filler track, this is the last Brian Wilson/Gary Usher song to be recorded and released by the Beach Boys (though the two would collaborate again in the 80s on some material, most of which was unreleased, but some sneaked out as very obscure Brian Wilson solo tracks).

A 12/8 ballad in the mould of *Tears On My Pillow* and similar 50s hits, this would have sounded dated even at the time – but Wilson and Usher were probably thinking of the string of Phil Spector songs about being too young to get married around this time (e.g. *Not Too Young To Get Married* by Bob. B. Soxx And The Blue Jeans, *Why Don't They Let Us Fall In Love* by Veronica (Ronnie Spector) and especially *So Young* by Veronica, which the band would cover on their next studio album). However, all these songs had more energy and seemed more up-to-date.

There's also an annoying bit of shoddy craftsmanship in that the second and third verses try to shove too many syllables into their first lines, forcing the band to come in slightly behind the beat after dropping out. This is especially noticeable at the start of the second verse ("They warned us that we can't live on love forever").

Brian's voice is also in his weakest point here – right at the top of his head voice where it turns into falsetto. When his voice started to deteriorate a few years later it was this range that went first, and this is the only range he's never really recovered. Here, it means he's drifting between a slightly off-pitch high head voice and a slightly nasal low falsetto more or less at random, occasionally singing in different 'voices' in each of his double-tracked vocals.

Carl's Big Chance

This is credited to Brian and Carl Wilson, but is in fact a filler instrumental whose backing track is clearly the vamp from Marvin Gaye's *Can I Get A Witness*, over which Carl plays some fairly rudimentary lead guitar – strangely sounding closer to Chet Atkins (albeit Chet Atkins as played by a teenager) than to the surf sounds on previous albums. Pointless.

Wendy

Another Wilson/Love lawsuit track, this is a very strong opener for side two of the original album. Other than its stuttering opening, and the studio noise (most notably a cough) heard during the Hammond solo, there's little to talk about here, but that's not to say it's not good – it's an excellent song, performed well, with a great lead by Brian. It's just that it's not a song that's improved by analysis – its good points are all obvious ones, and there's little to dig into below the surface.

Do You Remember?

This is Brian Wilson's tribute to the music he'd listened to growing up, and clearly based on *At The Hop*. Lasting barely a minute and a half (and that with an extended fade) there was clearly very little inspiration here. What's interesting about it (the only thing, really) is that this is rock nostalgia from before there was a 'canon' and official history of rock, as reported by someone who was a teenage music fan of the time. So in 'the guys who gave us rock & roll', along with Elvis, Little Richard and Chuck Berry we have the terminally uncool TV DJ Dick Clark and "Danny and the Juniors hit a groove, stuck as sharp as a knife".

Girls On The Beach

This is a rewrite by Brian of *Surfer Girl*, but a much less pleasant one – where *Surfer Girl* was a romantic song of love for one individual, this is attempting to give the same romantic feeling to a song which is lyrically not all that far removed in attitude from *Peaches* by the Stranglers – "The girls on the beach are all within reach if you know what to do" and "we love to lie around girls with tans of golden brown". It's not the sexist lyric itself that's the problem with this song – it's no worse in that respect than, say, *California Girls* – but it just doesn't go with the warm, romantic closely-harmonised melody. There's a cognitive dissonance there that there just isn't in *California Girls*' leering swagger. Lead vocals are by Brian, with Dennis on the middle eight.

Drive In

Another lawsuit-credited Wilson/Love song, with Mike on lead vocals, this is a comedy song of sorts, about teenage

ALL SUMMER LONG

life – the Drive-in is 'a groovy place to talk and maybe watch the show' when on a date, ("If you say you watch the movie you're a couple o' liars"), and how you shouldn't "sneak your buddies in the trunk 'cause they might get caught... And they'd look kinda stupid gettin' chased through the lot".

Love's vocal carries this off with the appropriate humour (and a wonderfully goofy Smokey Bear impression on "remember only you can prevent forest fires"), and the track, while not wonderful, is a pleasant improvement after the last two songs.

Incidentally, the Spectoresque backing track, one of the fullest arrangements on the album, was originally recorded several months earlier at the same session as the Christmas single *Little St Nick*, and a version of the backing track with the *Little St Nick* lyrics was released on the *Ultimate Christmas* compilation in the nineties. There's some debate about whether that version was intended as a joke, or whether two backing tracks were cut for the same lyric and the better one chosen. The presence of prominent sleigh bells on this leads me to suspect the latter.

Our Favourite Recording Sessions

This is filler. It's the equivalent of a film 'blooper reel', containing various breakdown takes and studio arguments (though only the more family-friendly ones – nothing like the argument over who spat in whose mouth that broke out during vocal overdubs on *Little Honda* for example). While other tracks have been relatively weak, this is the only real evidence that the band were still under immense pressure to crank material out by the yard.

Don't Back Down

And after a relatively weak run of songs, the album finishes with one of the best tracks .Written by Brian and (you guessed it) with a co-writing credit won by Mike in 1993, this is a reworking of *Hawaii* (with which the current touring 'Beach Boys' often perform this as a medley). It's very easy to imagine that on the choruses Brian is singing about himself when he sings "You gotta be a little nuts/but show 'em how you've got guts/Don't back down from that wave". Right now, Brian was feeling challenged by his rivalry with the Beatles (a rivalry which they had not yet noticed themselves, though they would by the next year), but soon the fear would start to take over... This was the last surf song the Beach Boys would record for four years.

CD Bonus tracks

Be True To Your School (single version)

A rerecording of this song, released as a single, it takes whatever simplistic charm the album version had, and bludgeons it to death, then runs over it with a steamroller to make sure. It takes the basic template of the album track, and adds a guitar solo, a marching band, an instrumental break to the tune of *On Wisconsin*, a cheerleading team (performed by The Honeys, a vocal group featuring Brian Wilson's fiancee, her sister and her cousin), a kitchen sink and Uncle Tom Cobbley and all.

All Dressed Up For School

This is absolutely astonishing. Between the opening *Louie Louie* riff with Mike Love's wonderfully stupid doot-doot-

doots and the closing *Papa Oom Mow Mow* bit, there are musical ideas here that would sustain many other bands for a lifetime – the verse melody was later recycled into two songs (*I Just Got My Pay* and *Marcella*), the chorus became a Honda commercial, the guitar solo seems to contain within it the seeds of the later hit *Dance, Dance, Dance*, part of the lyric was reused for *The Little Girl I Once Knew*, and a little bit of it at the end seems to point the way towards some of the *Smile* period *Heroes & Villains* vocal sessions. And it's a rare lead vocal at this point for Carl Wilson. So why wasn't it released?

With such a catchy chorus, you just can't help singing along...

>All dressed up for school
>
>Ooh what a turn on
>
>She's so fine
>
>What a turn on
>
>All dressed up for school

Ah.
 I see.
 Moving swiftly on...

Little Honda (Alternate Take)

This is almost indistinguishable from the released version, except for the backing vocal arrangement – instead of singing "Honda Honda going faster faster" they sing "Go little Honda, faster little Honda", and Brian's falsetto is more prominent. The change was an improvement. The only other change (changing the word 'champ', here, to 'matchless' in the finished version, presumably because Matchless is one of Honda's brand-names) was less so.

Don't Back Down (alternate take)

This is in many ways the most interesting of these bonus tracks, although musically the least listenable. It also provides quite a bit of justification for Mike Love's claim to have had input on at least this song. The backing track is identical to the finished version – obviously they kept the instrumental track – and the main theme of the lyrics is similar, but everything else is different. The melody here is actually the one Brian used for a song for The Honeys, *Hide Go Seek*, some time earlier, and the lyrics are totally different. Obviously the original idea was to reuse an unsuccessful but good song from a side project, before it was reworked in the studio. Given the speed with which Love has been known to work (writing lyrics in taxi-cabs to recording sessions on occasion) it wouldn't surprise me at all had he reworked the lyrics (though the new melody still has Brian's fingerprints all over it).

The Beach Boys' Christmas Album

One of two 'filler' albums released at the end of 1964 between proper studio albums, to capitalise on the band's popularity (the other being the *Beach Boys Concert* album) this appears to have been an attempt to position the band in a slightly more traditional, adult mode. The album is split into two sides, one 'rhythm' and one 'pops' as the phrasing of the time would have had it - or to put it another way, one side of rock & roll music for the teenagers and one side of heavily-orchestrated carols and standards for the grown-ups. This was a fairly standard technique at the time, and one can actually see something very similar happening with the tracklisting for *The Beach Boys Today!*

It should be remembered that at the time, rock & roll had been in the public eye for something less than ten years, so it was still entirely possible to dismiss it as a fad. The Beach Boys were taking sensible steps to have a long term career in case this guitar music thing stopped paying off.

The other notable thing about this album, though, is that it gave Brian a chance to work with Dick Reynolds, the arranger for Brian's idols the Four Freshmen, who arranged all of side two.

(A note about this album - it has been released on CD

many times - perhaps more than any Beach Boys album other than *Pet Sounds* - in various configurations. I am going to write here only about the album as originally released. The various bonus tracks will be taken care of with the *Ultimate Christmas* compilation, which I look at in volume two.)

line-up

Brian Wilson, Carl Wilson, Dennis Wilson, Mike Love, Al Jardine

Little Saint Nick

A rewrite of *Little Deuce Coupe*, with a little bit of *Car Crazy Cutie* thrown in (the move up a fourth for the middle eight and the repeated chanting), this was a Christmas hit in 1963, a year before the rest of the album was recorded. This version is the same recording as the single, but with the overdubs of tuned percussion, sleigh bells and so on removed, to make it fit better with the sound of the rest of side one (which was recorded in a hurry, and features only basic instrumentation). The song recasts Santa's sleigh as "the little Saint Nick", a vehicle to match any Cobra, Stingray or Deuce Coupe.

Love takes the lead, with Brian singing the falsetto "Merry Christmas Saint Nick" line. In its more fully-produced version this is a Christmas radio staple in the USA to this day. This is one of four songs on this album which Love won a co-writing credit for in his 1990s lawsuit.

The Man With All The Toys

Another hit single, this is the track on this side which has had the most effort expended on it, with Brian and Mike trading off lead lines and a lead guitar line that follows and comments on the vocal parts, as well as a brief *a capella* introduction/interlude. Amount of effort is, however, a relative thing on this album, and the song sounds bashed together quickly. Another one where Love won a co-writing credit.

Santa's Beard

A swing-time track in the mould of *Little Saint Nick*, but with a chord sequence closer to *She Knows Me Too Well* (see next album), this tale of taking a younger brother to see Santa at a department store, only to have ths sceptical sibling pull off Santa's beard is, with its *Jingle Bells* guitar solo and mocking chorus, easily the most enjoyable of these tracks. Another one where Love won a co-writing credit, Love takes lead here.

Merry Christmas, Baby

No relation to the Charles Brown classic of the same name, this is another swing-time song, this time with Love as a cheating boyfriend who has been dumped but wants to make up "if just for Christmas" and who seems oblivious to his own faults. A more subtle, and funnier, lyric than Love (assuming he was indeed the lyricist) was usually capable of, it seems that this album being a filler album allowed Love to try some new ideas (like the non-self-aware narrator here) which he wouldn't have risked on a 'proper' album. Another one where Love won a co-writing credit in his lawsuit.

Christmas Day

The only song on the album that remains a solo Brian Wilson songwriting credit, this is a notably clunkier lyric than the rest of the album, but has one of the better melodies, though is still fundamentally unmemorable. Al Jardine takes his first lead on this cheery track about how "it's worth the wait the whole year through/just to make happy someone like you" and does an excellent job.

Frosty The Snowman

And side one ends with a preview of side two, with this heavily-orchestrated version of the Christmas standard, with the band providing harmonies while Brian takes lead.

We Three Kings Of Orient Are

By far the best song on the album, this version of the old Christmas carol has the band singing in eerie block harmonies over a much darker arrangement than one would expect. An odd opener to side two, this is hauntingly beautiful.

Blue Christmas

This arrangement of the old standard is far too overdone, though, with Dick Reynolds coming across as a very low-rent Nelson Riddle, and the track's awash with harps, flutes and little tinkly things that have nothing to do with the mood of the song (though the quotes from *Rhapsody In Blue* on the instrumental break - presumably Brian's idea - are a nice touch). Brian manages an extremely good solo vocal on what is otherwise a fairly poor track.

Santa Claus Is Coming To Town

Done straight, rather than in the manner of Phil Spector's Christmas Album version with its additional chorus lines, this has Brian taking lead on the verses, with Mike singing "He sees you when he's sleeping".

White Christmas

Reynolds' over-lush style fits this standard rather better than it does many of the other songs on the album. Unfortunately, while the orchestration is OK and the band's harmonies are as good as ever, Brian's lead is the shoddiest bit of double-tracking I've heard from him.

I'll Be Home For Christmas

Reynolds still isn't restraining himself at all, but the band's block harmonies on this track make it worth a listen. This side of the album is getting awfully repetitive at this point, though, and just full of tinkling harps.

Auld Lang Syne

And the album finishes with a very nice *a capella* performance of this traditional song, with an overdubbed Christmas message from Dennis. The speed at which the band were working is apparent in the fact that Dennis flubs his words, and nobody bothered to record a second take. The harmonies are gorgeous though.

Today!/Summer Days... And Summer Nights!

Skipping, for the moment, the *Beach Boys Concert* album, we move on to the ninth album the band released in three years.

This is something that should be borne in mind when you read these essays, because from time to time I've been harsh on some of the songs. The fact is that in the first four years the band were together they recorded and released an astonishing eleven albums, and Brian Wilson had to write or co-write all the new material, do all the arrangements, produce and be one of the two lead singers.

The album we've skipped, for now, is *Beach Boys Concert*, which is paired on CD with another album from many years later, and doesn't add much to the story of the band's artistic progression.

The Beach Boys slowed down a little in 1965, 'only' recording three albums, including these two, two of their very best, but the pressure was beginning to show on Brian even so. He'd had his first nervous breakdown on a flight to the UK in November 1964, and had got married in December. Given the immense amount of new product he was under contract to produce, the fact that he was newly-married, and the toll touring was taking on his mental health, it's perhaps understandable that he decided to quit touring with the band.

The plan was that Brian would stay at home and write songs, and produce the backing tracks for the records using session musicians while the band were touring, and the band would come home and add vocals. Brian's place on tour was first taken by Glen Campbell – then one of LA's top session musicians, who would play on many of the band's recordings over the next few years, before he became famous in his own right as a singer – before Bruce Johnston replaced him.

Johnston was an experienced producer, songwriter, singer and keyboard player, best known at the time for his work with Terry Melcher on various projects. The biggest hit they'd worked on was *Hey Little Cobra*. Credited to The Rip-Chords, this was a Beach Boys/Jan & Dean knock-off (the chorus very similar to that of *Surf City*) that reached number four in the US charts. Johnston sang many of the harmony parts (most clearly it's him singing "Shut 'em down" in the choruses) so they knew he could handle the kind of material they were doing.

While Johnston wouldn't appear on the cover of a Beach Boys album until 1968, he started appearing on the recordings with *Summer Days...And Summer Nights!* and, apart from a few years in the mid-70s, has remained in the band ever since, and is still a member of the touring 'Beach Boys' to this day.

The Beach Boys Today!

Today! is widely considered one of the Beach Boys' very best albums – it's in Rolling Stone's 500 Best Albums Of All Time, Mojo's 1000 Albums You Should Own and all the other lists of that type. It's certainly the only one of the pre-*Pet Sounds* albums that I could almost unreservedly recommend to anyone. The run of studio albums *All Summer Long*, *Today!*, *Summer Days* are the peak of the early fun-in-the-sun Beach Boys albums, and of them all *Today!* is the most consistent.

It's also a turning point for the band's sound, recorded as it was right across the point where Brian quit the touring band. Thus there are tracks recorded almost as-live by just the band, tracks where the Beach Boys provide just vocals and tracks where the Beach Boys provide some instrumentation, augmented by the session musicians.

Brian Wilson used to draw from a fairly small pool of session players – the same people used by Phil Spector, for the most part – and so while there was no formal 'band', there were a group of musicians who would appear on many of these recordings, who were later nicknamed 'the Wrecking Crew'. Unless I say otherwise, when I refer to session players or 'the Wrecking Crew' in any of the essays on 60s albums, you can assume I mean some combination of:

Hal Blaine, Jim Gordon and/or Earl Palmer (drums – Blaine also would be the contractor, in charge of hiring the rest of the musicians), Carol Kaye and/or Ray Pohlman (bass), Jay Migliori, Steve Douglas and Plas Johnson (sax), Tommy Tedesco, Barney Kessel, Billy Strange and/or Glen Campbell (guitar, ukulele, banjo etc), Lyle Ritz (ukulele and occasional bass) Julius Wechter or Frank Capp (percussion) and Don Randi and/or Leon Russell (keyboards). Of the Beach Boys, Brian and Carl were most likely to add instruments to session tracks, with Bruce occasionally contributing and the others seldom.

This album is the first one where Brian appears to have paid attention to structuring it as an album – but even so, he's thinking in 1950s terms. Here he's following the structure of the Christmas album the band had just done in doing a side for 'the kids' (the uptempo, relatively simplistic, pop songs of the first side) and one for the 'grown-ups' (the harmonically sophisticated ballads of side two). Side two usually gets more recognition, as it's a pointer to the style used on *Pet Sounds*, but side one is also a marvel of pop music, with every song a potential or actual hit.

One final note before we move on to the track-by-track analysis – this album, more than any other, was involved in Mike Love's mid-90s lawsuit against Brian Wilson. Before then, the only track Love was a credited co-writer on was *Please Let Me Wonder* – now, all the original tracks here have Love as co-writer. These claims are still controversial among Beach Boys fans, but all I'll say is that while several songs definitely sound closer to Brian's lyrical style than Mike's, some of these songs have Mike Love's fingerprints all over them – I don't think anyone will deny, for example, that "Well since she put me down I've been out doin' in my head" might be the quintessential Mike Love line.

line-up

Brian Wilson, Carl Wilson, Dennis Wilson, Mike Love, Al Jardine

Do You Wanna Dance?

The album opens with a hit single, a cover of the Bobby Freeman song that in the Beach Boys' version reached number 12 in the US. Structurally, this is actually closer to Cliff Richard's 1962 cover version, which turned Freeman's tag into the chorus, than to the original, and it is this structure that has been covered by everyone from Bette Midler to John Lennon to The Ramones since. Dennis takes lead.

Good To My Baby

An example of the thicker production style Brian was now using, this is clearly influenced by Phil Spector, down to the prominent tambourine – this sounds like a girl-group song in the chorus, with the band singing in unison "she's my girl and I'm good to my baby". We could very easily imagine this being chanted by the Crystals or the Blossoms with only very slight lyrical alteration.

The *a capella* intro/break though is pure Beach Boys, with Mike singing the title in his lowest bass range, the band echoing him in the mid-range with Brian wailing a wordless falsetto on top, Carl or Dennis (I can't tell which) repeating the line, overlapping with the rest of the band, and Mike then repeating his original line two tones down. That break only lasts eight seconds, but it's eight seconds that mark this track as indelibly Beach Boys. Mike and Brian sing lead.

Don't Hurt My Little Sister

Another one with a chanted vocal chorus, this one was actually intended for Phil Spector to record.

In fact Spector recorded a backing track for the song but didn't add vocals. A couple of years later the track was released as *Things Are Changing For The Better* as a public service record for a government equality drive, with three different sets of vocals (by The Blossoms, Diana Ross & The Supremes and Jay & The Americans) being recorded for the same backing track. This version, however, contains the original lyrics, and while I'm trying not to go on too much about the soap operatic aspects of the band's life, the fact remains that this was inspired by something said to him by one of the Rovell sisters.

While Brian married Marilyn Rovell, he had at least a bit of romantic interest in her sister Barbara, and conducted an affair with her sister Diane through large parts of their marriage, so there's a very disturbing personal undercurrent to this song. That said, it sounds more like a companion piece to the previous song – almost as if the previous song (where "they think I'm bad and treat her so mean/but all they know is from what they've seen") was the defence of the callous boyfriend in this one – which it quite possibly was.

When I Grow Up (To Be A Man)

Apparently featuring only the Beach Boys plus a session harmonica player, this is an astonishingly complex and beautiful track, albeit with a fairly simply-structured song underneath. The drumming, in particular, sounds far more subtle than Dennis Wilson was usually capable of.

Another top-ten hit, this shows the questioning side of Brian's songwriting coming to the fore, with questions that everyone in their late teens and early twenties (as the band all were) must ask themselves – "will I look back and say that I wish I hadn't done what I did?" "Will my kids be proud or think their old man's really a square?"

While Brian was listening to Bach at this time, I suspect the prominent use of a harpsichord on this track has a slightly more prosaic inspiration – Brian's friends Jan & Dean had recently released as a single the deeply strange track *The Anaheim, Asuza And Cucamonga Sewing Circle, Book Review And Timing Association*, which used the instrument in a very similar way.

But the real joy of this track is in the melancholy fade. With the band chanting ever increasing numbers, Mike sings "Won't last forever" and Brian answers "It's kinda sad" with a gorgeous minor sixth chord under him. It's one of the first examples of Brian introducing totally new musical material in the fade, something that would show up later in the vocal rounds ending tracks like *God Only Knows* or *'Til I Die*.

That something as poignant as this could still be a hit single shows just how far Brian was able to go at this point without alienating the general public. Mike & Brian sing lead.

Help Me, Ronda

A different recording from the differently-spelled *Rhonda* that became a hit (which is on the next album), this one shows its roots in Buster Brown's *Fannie Mae* more clearly, with a harmonica part in the chorus that makes the connnection explicit. This is very similar to the single version, but slightly less thought-out, with a weird false fade that doesn't really work.

This was Al Jardine's second lead vocal for the band (after *Christmas Day* on the Christmas album) and it shows just how important his vocal contributions were. The only non-family member, he nonetheless had (and still has) a voice that is spookily like the rest of the band, especially Brian in the high range and Mike in the low, and he was not only probably the strongest singer in the band, but also had the widest range. While never as gorgeous a singer as Brian or Carl at their best, Al is in a real sense the voice of the Beach Boys in a way that none of the others are.

That *Fannie Mae* riff, incidentally, is one of the major themes that Brian returns to time and again over the next few years – you can hear it modified in such different tracks as *Salt Lake City* and *With Me Tonight*, and it becomes part of his musical toolkit in the same way as the intro to

Be My Baby or the *Shortenin' Bread* riff. But what's fascinating about this song in context is that despite it being on the surface a fairly jolly sort of song, it is, after all, a cry for help, repeated over and over again.

When John Lennon did this sort of thing a few months later people thought it was deep, but here it's just a Beach Boys pop song. At this point Brian was barely capable of writing anything that didn't have a dark undercurrent – a tendency that would become all the more prevalent over the next couple of years.

Dance, Dance, Dance

And having said that, of course, we get to the one utterly positive original song on the album. With a driving guitar riff apparently composed by Carl Wilson (who gets co-writing credit with Brian and, since the lawsuit, Mike), this is relatively simple musically (apart from the clever mid-verse semitone key change in the last verse (on the line "I play it cool when it's slow and jump it up when it's fast")) but succeeds by pure joie de vivre. Another top ten US hit, Mike and Brian sing lead.

Please Let Me Wonder

Starting side two, we get an immediate change of pace. Immediately we go into one of Brian and Mike's most beautiful ballads, full of uncertainty and doubt:

> Please let me wonder
>
> If I've been the one you love
>
> If I'm who you're dreaming of

We're seeing here again the recurring figure in Brian's songs of the man who knows he's not good enough for the wonderful woman he's with, and assumes she must realise this at some point but hopes not to be disillusioned just yet.

While clearly inspired by *Be My Baby*, though a much mellower, gentler song, this has a much lusher set of chord changes, which manage to cover quite a lot of harmonic ground while feeling like they're staying still, by moving one or two notes at a time, giving us wonderful chords like D#m(maj7)/D and F#maj9. Brian would later cover very similar musical ground with his 1977 song *Airplane*, but interestingly the song I know that's closest to this is actually *Something* by the Beatles.

The chord sequence for *Please Let Me Wonder* goes: I-Imaj7-I7-III-(-III/III♭)-ii7-V7. *Something*, on the other hand, goes I-Imaj7-I7-IV-II7-V7. Now, this isn't to say that George Harrison was ripping off Wilson – though he was aware of the song – both sequences, while interesting, are not hugely innovative, and I can easily see how a guitarist could come up with the *Something* sequence almost instinctively (it's a very natural set of movements for the fingers). And the pace is very different – Wilson covers this harmonic material in four bars while Harrison stretches it out to twelve. But it's still interesting how the Beach Boys could come up with something so similar to one of the Beatles' greatest records a full five years before their rivals. Brian and Mike sing lead, and both have only rarely been in better voice.

I'm So Young

A cover of an old doo-wop song, presumably influenced by the then-recent version by 'Veronica' (Ronnie Spector of the Ronettes) produced by Brian's idol Phil Spector. While it's a decent enough track, this is a bit of a retrograde step for the band, sounding more like *We'll Run Away* from *All*

Summer Long than the more sophisticated music around it.

Kiss Me Baby

One of the most glorious pieces of music the band ever made, the only bad thing I can say about this is that while the mono mix is of course gorgeous, this track is so musically dense that it's easy to miss individual moments of beauty, like the French horn under 'tossed and I turned, my head grew so heavy', or the single vibraphone notes at oddly appropriate spots.

Thankfully for those of us who study these things, a stereo remix was made available in 1999, and a vocal only mix in 2001. Thanks to these, we can make out individual parts (until the stereo remix, I'd never been able to figure out the backing vocals in the chorus – they're "kiss a little bit and fight a little bit and kiss a little bit"), and truly appreciate the craftsmanship that went into this.

Just as an example, Mike Love's vocal here is an astonishing piece of work, and has very obviously taken a huge amount of thought (whether by him or Brian). I single this out because Love often gets criticised for his vocals – and it's sometimes deserved, especially in live settings, when he's singing in his nasal tenor. But here he turns in the vocal of his career.

He sings in four distinct voices here. At the beginning, and in the verses, he's double tracked with a hell of a lot of reverb. It's a great double-tracking job by Love's standards up to then (the double-tracking on earlier albums had been very sloppy, because of the pressure they were under) – he matches himself in pronunciation and pitch precisely, even matching his breaths.

But he's singing in two distinct voices – one, the more prominent one, is his standard throat voice, while the other is an almost-whispered huskier throat voice. It almost sounds in fact like Dennis is double-tracking him here. This gives the vocal a strength, but with an undertone of hesitancy, that works perfectly for the lyric.

Then on the bridge, after Brian's line, we get him singing in his normal nasal head voice, again double-tracked, but this time so closely I had to listen to the *a capella* mix four times to decide if it was double-tracking or just reverb.

And then finally on the choruses he's down in his chest, singing the 'kiss a little bit and fight a little bit' in his bass voice.

The thing is, though, this isn't just a matter of range. All Love's vocal parts here take place in a very restricted range, and he could easily have sung the whole thing in no more than two 'voices' maximum. There's an attention to detail here in both arrangement and performance that borders on the obsessive, but it's produced one of the finest vocal performances I've ever heard. And Love was by most people's reckoning only the fourth-best singer in the band!

Surprisingly, this song seems to be based around a B-side instrumental Brian had written for another band, *After The Game* by The Survivors. While the chord changes are different, the first three notes of the melodies are the same and the guitar in the earlier song presages the 'kiss a little bit fight a little bit' parts of this song.

Lead vocals by Mike & Brian.

She Knows Me Too Well

The third world-class ballad on side two of *Today!*, this one suffers slightly in comparison with the other tracks, but that's only because we've already heard two of the best songs ever written. This one is 'merely' exceptionally good. Another song about a man who isn't good enough for his woman, this is the most blatant of Brian's songs about male vulnerability yet, and one of the most haunting:

> I treat her so mean, I don't deserve what I have
>
> And I think that she'll forget just by making her laugh
>
> But she knows me, knows me so well
>
> that she can tell
>
> I really love her

With a gorgeous lead vocal from Brian, this track apparently only features the Beach Boys instrumentally. And the quality of the performance should lay to rest any thoughts of it being incompetence on the band's part that led to the use of session players, rather than time pressure. Other than a couple of slightly stiff fills on the drums, this performance is every bit as good instrumentally as any of the others.

In The Back Of My Mind

And we finish the album as we start it, with a Dennis lead vocal. But this song couldn't be more different from *Do You Wanna Dance?*, being a slow ballad in 6/8 without any harmonies, and by far the most lushly orchestrated song on the album.

Even more explicitly about Brian's mental state than the previous track, the lyrics to this one are clearly personal:

> I'm blessed with everything
>
> In the world to which a man can cling
>
> So happy at times that I break down in tears

In the back of my mind I still have my fears

The chords here move obsessively around the same few tones, clustering in chords like A♭dim and B♭m6. Dennis, with his fragile voice, is the perfect vocalist for this track, and his practical breakdown at the end, on the words "it will always be in the back of my mind" as the track falls away into a dissonant string fade unlike anything in the rest of the track, is one of the best moments on the album, and it makes for a perfect ending for the album.

Bull Session With The Big Daddy

Unfortunately it isn't the end of the album, and we have the most bathetic piece of sequencing ever, as we go from that into two minutes and fourteen seconds of the band (plus Marilyn Wilson and journalist Earl Leaf) talking over each other while eating burgers and kosher pickles. Quite the most pointless thing in the band's discography.

Summer Days... And Summer Nights!

While *Today!* is considered a major step forward in the band's musical progression, *Summer Days* is usually regarded as, at best, a step sideways. In truth, this is unfair. The album suffers because *Today!* was such a massive leap forward while *Pet Sounds*, the next proper studio album, is The Greatest Album Ever Made And The Only Beach Boys Album You Should Own (copyright every music magazine ever). But in truth, there's not a single bad track on here, and it contains three of the band's biggest hits and one of Brian Wilson's greatest songs. Roughly contemporaneous with the Beatles' *Help!*, it's also of roughly that quality. Both albums are solidly good 60s pop with a few moments of brilliance, and any other band would have killed for an album like this in 1965.

While this is the first album to feature Bruce Johnston, Johnston was not credited as he was still signed to Columbia at the time. Al Jardine also didn't appear in the cover photo, due to illness. This was also the first album after Brian Wilson gained access to two things which would change the band's recordings forever – an eight-track recorder, and LSD.

line-up

Brian Wilson, Carl Wilson, Dennis Wilson, Mike Love, Al Jardine and Bruce Johnston (uncredited)

The Girl From New York City

This is an 'answer record' to the Ad Libs' hit *The Boy From New York City*. Based around the same riff, it has a different verse melody and lyrics, but the inspiration is clear. A simple, fun, dance tune, the main point of interest is Mike Love's delightfully dumb bass vocals. This is a song where Mike Love won co-writing credit in 1993. Love sings lead on the verses. The choruses are sung by the group, but with Carl's voice most prominent.

Amusement Parks USA

This is one of the few actual backwards steps on the album. Based around Freddie 'Boom Boom' Cannon's hit *Palisades Park*, this is essentially a reworking of *County Fair* from the *Surfin' Safari* album, but with the addition of a list of place names (Mike Love seems to have become convinced that this is the secret to commercial success after *Surfin' USA*). The soundscape gives a better sense of place than the earlier record (and Hal Blaine is quite risque for the time with his turn as a carnival barker advertising "Stella the snake dancer.... she's got the biggest asp in town"), but it's filler, albeit enjoyable, well-crafted filler. Another one that Love won co-writing credit for, Love and Brian Wilson share the lead vocals here.

Then I Kissed Her

A cover version of the Crystals track, written by Jeff Barry, Ellie Greenwich and Phil Spector, and originally produced by Spector and arranged by Jack Nitzsche. Other than the gender re-write, which also changes the protagonist from being passive to active ("Then he kissed me" becomes "Then I kissed her"), the track sticks very closely to the original.

The main differences are that Brian gets rid of the superfluous string section (the one bit of interesting melodic material the original string part had is replicated on a Hammond organ), and he provides a full, though rudimentary, backing vocal arrangement (mostly just 'ooh' chords – still more than the Crystals had, where the backing vocalists were limited to doubling Darlene Love on the title phrase).

They also cut the instrumental break and superfluous repeat of the middle eight and final verse.

Al Jardine takes the lead here and does a sterling job, his vocal easily better than that of Darlene Love on the original (and that's saying something – Love was one of the best session singers of the time). The end result is a refinement and improvement on the original, already a very fine single. This was released as a stopgap single two years later, in a very different marketplace, and still managed a very respectable number four in the UK charts.

Salt Lake City

Another one for which Love won co-writing credit, this one is a simple little rocker, driven by a neat doubled-up four-note phrase on guitar and bass. But listen for when the instrumental break starts – the sax is playing a variant of the *Fannie Mae/Help Me, Rhonda* riff, which continues through the rest of the song. This variant would return as late as Brian's 2004 album *Gettin' In Over My Head*, where the same sax part is used to drive *Desert Drive*.

Lyrically, the song is pretty standard fare, except I find it hard to believe that even by 1965 standards Salt Lake City, the home of Mormonism, had 'the grooviest kids'. Mike and Brian share lead.

Girl Don't Tell Me

Despite his avowed preference for Paul McCartney's work, Brian Wilson seems to me to be far closer as a songwriter to John Lennon. Both have the same lyrical themes, both structure their songs around chord changes and harmonies rather than primarily around melody, both use lots of leaps into falsetto and small stepwise movements, rather than jumps within the same range.

Certainly, when the band came to record the stopgap *Beach Boys Party!* album, the three Beatles songs they covered (*Tell Me Why*, *I Should Have Known Better* and *You've Got To Hide Your Love Away*) were all Lennon songs as was the fourth, unreleased, cover, *Ticket To Ride*. And *Ticket To Ride* is the crucial one here.

Brian has claimed this was 'written for the Beatles', but he presumably means it was inspired by them – specifically, it's very obviously written off the back of *Ticket To Ride*. Quite possibly this was Brian feeling the same urge that drove Paul McCartney to write *That Means A Lot* –

SUMMER DAYS... AND SUMMER NIGHTS! 79

the urge to add more chord changes to a song which has none in its first ten bars. But whereas *That Means A Lot* keeps *Ticket To Ride*'s dark, ponderous production, this goes to the opposite extreme and is light and breezy as a feather.

The whole thing is very, very clearly modelled on its inspiration. The celesta figure (played by Johnston, in his first recording session with the group) is essentially an anagram of the guitar riff from the Beatles song, the vocal melodies start out almost identically, and most obviously the chorus – "Girl don't tell me you'll wri-i-ite" repeated three times followed by "me again this time" is almost fingerprint identical to that of *Ticket To Ride*.

There are other, more general, Lennonisms scattered throughout the song as well – 'gu-u-uy' and 'ti-i-ime' both seem to be copying Lennon's copies of Smokey Robinson (e.g, *Not A Second Time*). The whole effect is very different from any other Beach Boys track of the time, especially since it features a solo vocal with no backing vocals, and that vocal is by Carl Wilson, who had only ever taken two leads before (*Pom Pom Play Girl* and *Louie Louie*). Carl clearly sounds hesitant here, and there's no hint that within a year he'd have become one of the greatest vocalists in rock history.

It's also a surprisingly sparse backing track, featuring only the Wilson brothers (on acoustic guitar, bass and drums) plus Johnston and a session tambourine player, and sounds like it was cut more-or-less live, with only the slashed electric guitar chords on the chorus being overdubbed.

If the song doesn't rise to its inspiration's emotional intensity, in some ways that's a good thing – it's hard for Brian to write that kind of song because he's neither as fundamentally selfish nor as misogynist as Lennon was at that time. Even so, this song is fascinating as the most blatant example of the trans-Atlantic creative dialogue between the two bands that would heat up over the next eighteen months.

Help Me, Rhonda

This is a remake of the track from *Today!*, and this is the version that got to number one. Comparing the two versions shows how Brian would refine his musical ideas. Rather than starting with the ukulele intro, this comes straight in with "Well since she put me down...", backed by bass and percussion, before the rest of the instruments come in. Carol Kaye's bassline is far more prominent here, and a much better part, with a strong jazz influence — one of the first of the truly great bass parts that Brian would come up with over the next couple of years.

Mike's bass vocal part has been completely rewritten — the "bow bow bow" and "come on Rhonda" parts that are such a crucial part of the song's appeal only show up here. The harmonica, if it's there at all, is submerged in a horn section and the drums don't overpower the rest of the instruments.

Rather than an instrumental break consisting of just the track without vocals, here we have a properly thought out break, a brief dialogue between boogie piano and electric guitar. And finally, instead of the annoying, overlong, fake fade on the chorus from the original version, we have a short instrumental fade on a repeat of the main riff.

While to a casual listener the two tracks are fairly similar — in fact the original version was included on the multi-platinum hits compilation *Endless Summer* in the 70s without many listeners even noticing — a comparison of the two shows the difference between a filler album track and a massive hit single.

This version still features Al Jardine on lead vocals, and reached number one in the US (knocking *Ticket To Ride* off after one week – the shortest time a Beatles record had had at the top of the charts up to that point) – the band's second of four US number one hits.

California Girls

This song is a difficult one to talk about, because its problematic aspects make it hard to hear just how good it actually is. The lyric (for which Mike Love won songwriting credit in the 90s, and which definitely sounds like Love's work to me – a string of placenames with a bit of leering on top) is dull-witted and unpleasant, and Love's nasal vocal doesn't really sell it.

But ignoring that, there's a lot to love here. It says a lot about the kind of songwriter Brian Wilson is that this was the result of his first LSD trip, the music being written while he was on acid. Inspired by the intervals and general feel of *Jesu, Joy Of Man's Desiring* (another of the many pieces that haunt the band's career), Wilson and Love turn it into a celebration of a rather more secular kind of joy.

The most striking part of the track is, of course, the intro – a simple, repeated, nine-note phrase, slowly building up with the addition of instruments. Starting out with just 12-string guitar, within its twenty-two seconds it adds organ, trumpet, two saxes, bass, cymbal and vibraphone, to create a unique instrumental texture unlike anything else. (Just a shame about the studio chatter that makes it onto the very end of the intro. While in every other way a perfectionist, Wilson was never the best about ensuring his tapes were free of studio noise).

The driving force of much of the rest of the song is Carol Kaye and Lyle Ritz's bassline, revolving for almost all the time around the notes B, F# and G, and the band's vocals.

This was the first track to feature Bruce Johnston on vocals (he can clearly be heard singing the answering "wish they all could be California" in the chorus – one of the most prominent vocal parts he takes on a well-known Beach Boys track), and also one of the first for which the vocals were recorded on eight-track, allowing them to triple-track all the vocals. This means that while previous Beach Boys tracks tended to feature just the five Beach Boys singing live plus usually the lead singer double-tracked, this has a full eighteen voices on it, giving the harmonies a thicker texture they'd never had before.

And those harmonies are astonishing. They're low in the mix, but listen to the backing vocals under "I dig a French bikini on Hawaiian island dolls" – those block harmony "ooh-wah-ooh-wah-ooh-wah-ooh-wah-aah" parts are as good as any vocals ever recorded. On its release this went to number three in the US charts, and it's still one of the band's most popular tracks.

Lead vocals are by Mike Love on the verses, with Brian and Bruce Johnston on the choruses.

Let Him Run Wild

Supposedly inspired by Burt Bacharach, this actually has very little similarity to his work, being harmonically and rhythmically very simplistic, consisting for the most part of a shuffle between i7 and iv7 (or vi7 and ii7 – I'm not sure whether to consider this as being in D#m or F#, its relative major). Harmonically, there's little here that anyone couldn't write (I could knock out similar chord changes in a few minutes, as could any semi-competent songwriter). This one, again, Love claimed co-writing credit for in 1993.

What makes the track work — and it's easily the best track on the album — is the arrangement. Every instrument here is made to sound unlike itself. The piano part is actually, if you listen to the isolated instrumental track (available on the Stack O' Tracks album) a tack piano doubled with a vibraphone and with some hand percussion playing at the same time in the same range.

The guitar is played through a Leslie speaker (something the Beatles didn't start to do until *Revolver*, nearly a year later). The instruments are used in ways that go completely contrary to their normal rock usage as well. The guitar, which would normally be the lead instrument, instead just repeats a four-note phrase (this use of the guitar paves the way for the track *Pet Sounds* next year).

The bass, on the other hand, which would normally be plodding along with the four-on-the-floor feel of the piano part, is instead playing a fluid contrapuntal melody — one that changes and gets more complex as the song goes on. If you want to hear why Paul McCartney's basslines suddenly got interesting in 1966, this song (and others like it) is why.

The drums, which only come in on the bridge to the first chorus, aren't used to keep time but to punctuate the end of the bass phrases. The only instruments that are used in their normal way are the horns, and the backing track for the chorus sounds more than anything like the Count Basie band, a straight horn-driven slightly bluesy swing piece. I could easily hear Ella Fitzgerald or Ray Charles singing lead on this.

But Brian's lead vocal on this track is astonishing. Unfortunately, he doesn't think so himself — he kept it off the 1993 5-CD retrospective *Good Vibrations: Thirty Years Of The Beach Boys* (making it, along with *Don't Talk (Put Your Head On My Shoulder)* one of only two essential Beach Boys tracks not on that superb collection) because he thought his voice sounded effeminate. But it's an absolute *tour de force*. Singing mostly right at the top of his tenor range, occasionally shading over into falsetto in the verses, on the choruses, while the band sing the main melody, he hits some of the highest notes of his career as he practically screams "Let him run!" Easily the masterpiece of the album, this is one of the greatest tracks of the band's career.

You're So Good To Me

Another disputed co-write, listening to this and the previous song back to back it's hard to believe they're the work of the same band, let alone that they have the same lead vocalist. But actually, this song helps tie the album together neatly. Like *Girl Don't Tell Me* it's a take-off on a rival band, this time the Four Seasons with their Motown-esque four-on-the-floor stampers. Like *Let Him Run Wild* it's structured round two-bar crotchet phrases with simple chord changes and features a guitar put through a Leslie speaker. And it has some harmonic similarities to *The Girl From New York City*. Here it's all put in service of a Motown-style stomper, with Brian's vocals being the closest he ever came to being a conventional rock singer, and with some delightfully goofy "duh duh duh" backing vocals from Love. This might only be a minor track, but it's a wonderfully enjoyable one, and if I had to choose one track to sum up this album it would be this one.

Summer Means New Love

While previous Beach Boys instrumentals had been dull Dick Dale pastiche, this one is a very different beast. Melodically owing a little to *Graduation Day* by the Four Freshmen in the middle eight, and stylistically similar to Brian's earlier *After The Game*, this little piece of semi-exotica owes most to the instrumentals on *The Lonely Surfer* by Jack Nitzsche (Phil Spector's arranger and later an Oscar-winning film composer), especially *Theme From A Broken Heart*. While this is more romantic and less bombastic than Nitzsche, who could do subtle but always preferred to have half a dozen kettle drums bashed at full volume, the inspiration is clear. More than any other track on the album, this points the way forward to what Brian would be doing on *Pet Sounds* a few months later.

I'm Bugged At My Old Man

And from the sublime to the ridiculous, we get this comedy song. Just Brian at the piano, with the other band members adding backing vocals, this is possibly the first thing the Beach Boys did that could be described as 'outsider music', as much of their mid-70s stuff was, though this is still more knowing than that material.

Over a twelve-bar blues played in the style of Fats Domino, Brian sings, sometimes in a parody Elvis voice, about how he's been locked in his room by his dad for being suspended from school ("I ripped up my wardrobe and I'm growing a beard/Oh when will they let me come out?"). While the punishments here are comically exaggerated, and the song is all in good fun, there's more than a hint of truth behind it, and Brian occasionally sounds almost sincere. This is the last of the comedy interludes on Beach Boys records, and has the virtue of being a proper song of sorts, but it's also quite painful if you actually know anything of Brian's personal history. I suspect it's a case of having to laugh to keep from crying...

And Your Dream Comes True

And the album finishes with one of the lovely little fragments that are scattered about the Beach Boys' career. This is an *a capella* piece, just 63 seconds long. In Four Freshmen style harmony, this is a slowed down version of *Baa Baa Black Sheep*, but with four lines of lyric:

> You're so sleepy, wish that he could stay
>
> Love him so but now it's getting late
>
> He'll be waiting, waiting just for you
>
> One more summer and your dreams come true

Surprisingly moving.

CD Bonus tracks

The Little Girl I Once Knew

A non-album single that 'only' reached number 20 in the US chart, its relative lack of success is generally put down to the fact that between the verses and choruses there are two bars of silence, and DJs don't like 'dead air'.

In fact, I suspect its relative failure is down to it sounding like an attempt to write *California Girls Part II*. It has a similar rhythmic feel, another (less successful) slow-build instrumental intro, and another chorus where Brian and Bruce sing the title in call-and response fashion. It's structurally almost identical to the earlier song, other than the 'lah doo day' interlude, but less subtle, with a kitchen-sink approach that suggests Brian had been paying too much attention to Spector.

It's an enjoyable enough single, but its reputation among Beach Boys fans as an unappreciated masterpiece owes

CD BONUS TRACKS

far more to its chart position than to its quality. Had it been a massive hit, no-one would think anything of it. It is, however, unusual in that it's the only Beach Boys hit single never to have been included on an album.(The hit version of *Cottonfields* wasn't included on a US album, but was on the UK version of *Sunflower*). It was probably originally intended for the album that became *Pet Sounds*, but by the time that album was being sequenced it was obvious it didn't fit.

Dance, Dance, Dance (alternate take)

An early version of the song, featuring just the Beach Boys themselves performing. Fairly similar to the released version, except that the guitar solo clearly hasn't been worked out properly, and the tambourine on the chorus seems almost to drown everything else out.

I'm So Young (alternate take)

An early, slightly-sloppily-doubly-tracked, vocal take over the same backing track as the released version. Almost indistinguishable from the released version.

Let Him Run Wild (alternate take)

Again, nearly identical to the released version, this has a different vocal part on the chorus – "Let him run wild he don't care baby" instead of "Let him run wild he don't care", and the additional word 'so' before the word 'before' in the second verse. If you hadn't heard the finished version, you'd think this was wonderful, but the chorus was hugely improved by the change.

Graduation Day

A studio run-through, with just vocals and a single electric guitar, of a Four Freshmen ballad that was a staple of the band's live set at the time. Being British, I haven't had the American High School experience that this song is about, so perhaps for those who have it would give a very different impression. But to me this is fairly dull kitsch, redeemed only by some very good vocals.

Beach Boys Party!/Stack O' Tracks

Where other albums have filler tracks, this is an entire filler CD.

Of the two albums on this CD, one, 1968´s *Stack-O-Tracks* consists entirely of instrumental mixes of tracks from previous records, so I won't be dealing with it at all here – all I'd be saying is "It's *Darlin'* without the vocals – see the entry for *Darlin'* under the *Wild Honey* album."

The other album, though, *Beach Boys Party!*, requires at least a cursory glance through.

Beach Boys Party!

Unlike the albums that surround it, *Beach Boys Party!* is as far from being a complex, heavily-orchestrated masterpiece as possible. The band's next real album, *Pet Sounds* would not be ready for several more months, but Capitol Records wanted a Christmas cash-in release.

The two obvious ideas – a live album and an album of Christmas songs – had both been done the year before. So this time, it was decided to record a 'live-in-the-studio' album as if it were recorded at a party the band were attending,

So the band got together in the studio with a few acoustic guitars and Hal Blaine on bongos, and knocked out a set of incredibly sloppy cover versions of songs chosen seemingly at random, and then got friends to add party noises, and added a few wild tracks of party effects. This means that even the better tracks on the album have mistakes left in and general chatter and noise over the top.

The album might well have made a great soundtrack to a teenager's party in 1965 – and even today for that matter – but as music, as a listening experience, it ranges from pretty decent to outright horrible, and tends towards the latter.

line-up

Brian Wilson, Carl Wilson, Dennis Wilson, Mike Love, Al Jardine and Bruce Johnston (uncredited) Also features – Marilyn Wilson (backing vocals), Dean Torrence (vocals), Hal Blaine (percussion), Billy Hinsche (harmonica)

Hully Gully

A song originally recorded by The Olympics in 1959, this starts the album as it means to go on – a fun party tune with silly lyrics. Generally speaking, the album is split between songs that the band knew as teenagers (like this one) and ones by their contemporary influences. A nothing tune in this version, the original by the Olympics is a nice, strutting R&B track in the style of the Coasters, with a laid-back groove totally missing from this version. Mike takes lead.

I Should Have Known Better

The first of three Beatles covers on the album – all covers of Lennon songs (lending credence to my belief that Lennon, rather than McCartney, is the closer songwriter to the Beach Boys' style). This features just the first two verses and middle eight of the song, sung in unison by several people. At various points the most prominent voice in the mix is Al (always the strongest vocalist in the band), Brian or Brian's wife Marilyn (a singer herself, with girl-group the Honeys, though not a particularly good one). Mike tries to add some character with some "bow bow bow" backing vocals in the middle eight, but this is just a crowd singing along with an acoustic guitar...

Tell Me Why

The second Lennon cover, this is a more creditable performance, as the song's simple block harmonies and four-chord changes make it perfect for this kind of atmosphere – especially since the band don't bother with the instrumental intro from the original (like the previous song, on the *A Hard Day's Night* album). Even so, the performance falls apart at the end of the middle eight like before. I'm still unsure who's singing lead here – Wikipedia says Carl and Al, and it could be them – but it could also be Brian and Carl or Brian and Al. No matter how many times I listen (and I've listened multiple times just now to the finished version and to two outtakes) I can't decide for sure – this is in precisely the range where those three sound most similar.

In a nice touch, Brian added this to the acoustic 'party' set when he performed in Liverpool in 2004 on the Smile tour, in this arrangement (such as it is).

Papa-Oom-Mow-Mow

The best track so far, this was actually the second time the band had recorded this song, originally by The Rivingtons, in a year – it had appeared on the *Concert* album the previous year. This is actually the better of the two versions, because the fun in this song is almost entirely in the vocal performance – Love growling the 'papa oom mow mow' part in a comically low bass voice, while Brian screeches, yowls, whoops and wails in falsetto. The looseness of this setting allows them to go to ridiculous extremes with this, and the result is genuinely enjoyable.

Mountain Of Love

Originally by Harold Dorman, a one-hit wonder, this had been a hit the previous year for Johnny Rivers, and it's Rivers' arrangement the Beach Boys are clearly copying here, down to the backing vocals. A simple twelve-bar blues with little going for it, the song obviously stuck with Brian Wilson – twelve years later he copied the middle eight note for note for his song *Little Children* (which remained unreleased for another eleven years and eventually became a track on his first solo album).

Love sings lead, and rudimentary harmonica is provided by Billy Hinsche, of the minor teen-pop band Dino, Desi and Billy. Carl Wilson would marry Hinsche's sister Annie the next year, and Hinsche became a regular member of the Beach Boys' touring band from the early 70s, adding keyboards, guitar and backing vocals until the mid-90s.

You've Got To Hide Your Love Away

The third Lennon cover on the album, and one of only two tracks that could really be counted as in any way good here, Dennis takes lead and plays the song straight (though the party crowd do all join in on the "Hey!" parts). While it's spoiled by the party noises (this is anything but a party song), Dennis' soulful croak is perfect for this song, one of Lennon's best and most mournful. It also, more than any of the other tracks, puts the lie to the ostensibly spontaneous nature of these recordings – Dennis is very sloppily double-tracked here. This song actually entered the band's setlist as Dennis' vocal spot (taking over from *The Wanderer*).

If you want to hear just how good the song sounds without the party noises, at least three concerts featuring the song have been widely bootlegged (two from Michigan in excellent quality soundboard recordings, one from Japan as an audience recording with some nice added harmonies), not that I could ever recommend taking such action of course, but even here this is far and away the best thing on the album so far.

Devoted To You

And this is the best thing on the album full stop. A rather light little ballad written by Felice and Boudleaux Bryant for the Everly Brothers, here Mike and Brian sing it, with Carl accompanying on the guitar, and they are absolutely stunning.

While the Everlys are possibly the greatest vocal harmony duo of all time, *Devoted To You* isn't one of their better efforts – giving the melody to Phil while Don sang low harmony (usually Don would sing melody while Phil would take high harmony) means it doesn't play to their strengths. On the other hand here Brian and Mike still have the vocal similarity that comes from being family members, but Brian gets to sing the song in a gorgeous falsetto while Mike harmonises in a rich baritone.

Off the top of my head I can't think of another time when Brian and Mike have harmonised so closely – the signature Beach Boys style required the two of them to be almost antiphonal, playing off each other while the rest of the band did block harmonies in the middle. And later on, of course, the band moved away from harmony to a great extent and towards counterpoint. But this shows how much this was a conscious choice – these two voices, alone, are absolutely spellbinding. Much as I love Brian's more complex vocal arrangements, I'd still kill to hear an album of Brian and Mike singing two-part harmony *a la* Simon & Garfunkel, the Everlys or the Louvin Brothers. The party noises are mixed down for this one, but if you want to give the track the respect it deserves, the rarities CD *Hawthorne, CA* has a mix of this with the noises mixed out altogether.

Alley Oop

Originally a country single for Dallas Frazer, this song about the cartoon caveman had become a hit for the Hollywood Argyles in 1960. The Hollywood Argyles were a studio creation put together by Kim Fowley (a schoolfriend of Bruce Johnston who managed to be involved in a minor way in almost every major music event for thirty years despite having no discernible talent – he made some of the first surf records, played on Frank Zappa's first album, is the announcer on John Lennon's *Live Peace In Toronto* and so on – he's the LA hipster equivalent of Zelig) and their take on the song was essentially to turn it into *Hully Gully* (and indeed they had a hit with a cover of that song in 1961).

BEACH BOYS PARTY!

This is also (along with *The Monster Mash*) one of two songs the Beach Boys covered which were also covered by the Bonzo Dog Band, who presumably came across both songs from the Beach Boys' versions.

I mention all this because there's little to say about the song itself, which is just *Hully Gully* with lyrics about dinosaurs.

There's No Other (Like My Baby)

A four-chord doo-wop ballad written by Phil Spector and Leroy Bates for the Crystals, this is played fairly straight, sticking close to the template of the original record, with Brian singing the Darlene Love lead part, and the rest of the band and 'party guests' singing the unison vocal choruses. Other than *You've Got To Hide Your Love Away* and *Devoted To You* this is the most straightforward, respectful cover on the album. Unfortunately, it's a straightforward, respectful cover of a plodding dirge, but you can't have everything.

I Get Around/Little Deuce Coupe

A 'hilarious' comedy medley of two of the Beach Boys' own hits, where Mike Love tries to improvise funny parody lyrics and fails miserably. An example is that after one of the "I get around" bits he sings "square". Oh my aching sides.

The Times They Are A-Changin'

Al Jardine, the band's resident folkie, here gets a chance to sing a Dylan song. One always gets the impression from Jardine, with his whitebread earnestness, that he wishes he'd been in one of the bands parodied in *A Mighty*

Wind – whereas Brian Wilson obsessed over the Four Freshmen, Jardine was a Kingston Trio fan, and his later contributions to the band are often either attempts at protest songs (*Lookin' At Tomorrow*, *Don't Go Near The Water*) or clean-cut versions of old folk songs (*Sloop John B* and *Cottonfields*. It tells you everything you need to know about Jardine that it was his idea to do Sloop John B but that at the recent reunion performance he added "but not too much!" after the line "drinkin' all night").

Jardine obviously likes the song, and does a very creditable job, punctuated by random shouts from the crowd, who seem less than impressed.

Barbara Ann

Oh dear... Dean Torrence, of Jan & Dean, was known as a nice person.

However, it was equally well known that he couldn't carry a tune in a bucket, even if that bucket were inside another bucket with an easy-carry handle, and if he were aided by two professional bucket-carriers and a bucket-carrying machine. He sometimes wasn't even allowed to sing on Jan & Dean's own records, the falsetto parts being as likely to be sung by Brian Wilson or P.F. Sloan as by Torrence himself.

Nonetheless, he was there in the studio, and it was decided that he'd be allowed to sing lead on this, a cover of a song written by Fred Fassert for The Regents, which Jan & Dean had recently covered themselves. After all, this was a filler album, no-one was going to pay attention, right?

Carl Wilson, thirty-one years later, called this song "the bane of my life". Released as a single by the record company without the band's knowledge or permission, this sloppy, hideously off-key (Dennis can be heard during a session

BEACH BOYS PARTY! 97

outtake groaning "Hey Dean, sing on key! Jesus!") cover version, where the band forget the words half-way through and with someone who isn't even in the band on lead vocals, somehow became one of their biggest ever hits, and they had to sing it every working day for the rest of their lives. Just goes to show that you should never just pump out filler crap for the money, or it can come back to bite you...

Pet Sounds

And so we get to the most difficult Beach Boys album for me to write about. Not because it's musically more difficult than any other album, but because it's much harder to find new things to say about it.

While I only know of a tiny number of books that deal with the Beach Boys' music in any detail, I own two books devoted to this single album (those by Charles Granata and Kingsley Abbot, to both of which I have referred during writing this). Before I carry on, if you want to know precisely which version I'm listening to and why, skip to the bottom.

Brian Wilson's life went through a massive change in 1965. In very late 1964 he'd both had his first nervous breakdown and got married, and then in 1965 he tried LSD for the first time, quit touring with the rest of the band, and got access to an eight-track recorder for the first time. He'd already recorded one album – *Summer Days* – using predominantly studio musicians, but with the album that became *Pet Sounds* he was going to come close to recording a solo album, using the other band members as only vocalists (and often only backing vocalists at that).

Brian had heard the Beatles album *Rubber Soul* (not the original UK version but the revised US tracklisting) and become enraptured with the idea of recording "a whole album with all good stuff" – it having not occur ed to him previously that you could record an album with no filler.

To help him write this album he turned, not to any of his previous collaborators, but to Tony Asher, an advertising copywriter with no previous experience of professional songwriting. The two of them would sit in Brian's house, talking about Brian's emotions, and then they would write the most personal songs Brian had ever written up to that point.

This should be remembered when one reads comments about Mike Love allegedly disliking *Pet Sounds* originally, which he denies. Up to that point, Love had effectively been the co-leader of the band. He was the frontman, wrote the bulk of the lyrics, and sang the bulk of the lead vocals, while Brian wrote the music, produced the records and sang a minority of the leads.

Now there was an album which was not only stylistically different from everything they'd done before, but on which he got two lead vocals and almost no songwriting input. *Pet Sounds* is indubitably a masterpiece, but it's Brian Wilson's masterpiece, not a Beach Boys masterpiece, and one can hardly blame Love for being annoyed at being reduced to a sidekick for his cousin, especially when his livelihood was on the line.

In the event, *Pet Sounds* was hardly the commercial failure it has later been made out to be – it was a top ten album in both the US and the UK, and contained four top forty singles (*Sloop John B*, *Wouldn't It Be Nice/God Only Knows*, the two sides of which charted separately in the US, and *Caroline, No* which made the charts in the US as a solo single for Brian Wilson). It did, however, mark the point at which the band's commercial fortunes in its home country began to wane – even as it also marked the real beginning of their commercial and critical success elsewhere.

While within eighteen months of *Pet Sounds'* release

the Beach Boys would be washed up in their home country, the influence the album had on, especially, the Beatles, meant that the band's future as critical darlings was assured in the UK and Europe.

On remastering

It's difficult to know that the reader is listening to the same recording as I am – *Pet Sounds* having been reissued, remastered, and generally messed-around with more than any other album I own. It was issued on CD in 1990, in a rather flat mix with a ton of noise reduction, making for a listenable CD but with little top end. A *Pet Sounds Sessions* box set came out in 1997, with a newly remastered version with no noise reduction (which I personally find unlistenable due to the tape hiss) but with a brilliantly clear new stereo mix (which crucially missed a few overdubs) and with tons of session recordings.

Another CD issue came out in 2001, with yet another remastering job on the mono mix and a slightly altered stereo mix (including some but not all of the formerly-missing overdubs). And yet another CD version came out in 2006... (that's not to mention the live CD of Brian Wilson performing the entire album live, or the live DVD...) For discussions of this album I will be using the mono version in the 2001 master. To hear significant details, however, you may well want to listen to the isolated backing tracks, isolated vocals, outtakes, alternate versions and session recordings on The *Pet Sounds Sessions* box set.

line-up

Brian Wilson, Carl Wilson, Dennis Wilson, Mike Love, Al Jardine and Bruce Johnston (uncredited). All songs by

Brian Wilson and Tony Asher except where mentioned.

Wouldn't It Be Nice

The opening song of the album doesn't stray too far from 'the formula', being a wistful love song that could, lyrically, be considered as following straight on from the last song on the band's previous studio album – going from "he'll be waiting, waiting just for you, one more summer and your dream comes true" to "Wouldn't it be nice if we were older, and we wouldn't have to wait so long?" is really no jump at all.

Musically, however, this is very different from anything the band had done previously – the only guitars one can hear are on the intro (yes, that is a guitar, played by Jerry Cole) and on the middle eight (where the same figure is doubled by Al de Lory on piano). There is apparently a second guitar on the track, played by Bill Pitman, but I don't hear it.

Instead, we have something akin to *California Girls* in the way it uses whole-step chord differences – you can take individual lines from the two songs and sing them over each other, though not in the same order – but with a far more staccato rhythm that would become, in the mind of many people, a trademark of the Beach Boys' mid-60s sound.

While Brian rarely used that rhythm again, so many people copied this (starting with *Penny Lane*, which is very much McCartney trying to remake this specific track) that the feel of the track became a cliché. Even so, though, most people, when they're going for that rhythm, do so with straight piano chords. Here, on the other hand, we have the rhythm track played by two accordions, an organ, and two mandolins – a standard eight-string one and a custom twelve-string. (The 'strings' on the middle eight are also accordion, played with extra vibrato).

Meanwhile, rather more subtly, the song sets up the tertian movements that will recur throughout the album – we start in A for the intro, move down a third to F for the first verse, then down a minor third to D for the middle eight. In a very real sense, then, this song is the bridge between *Summer Days* (with its juvenile themes and its musical similarity to *California Girls*) and the rest of *Pet Sounds*.

Brian takes lead, with Mike singing the first two lines of the middle eight and the 'good night baby' tag. (Mike's middle eight vocal part is missing from the stereo mix on the box set, replaced by Brian, but is there on later stereo remixes).

This song is the most controversial of all those over which Mike Love sued in the 1990s. While no-one disputed that he had co-written, for example, *California Girls*, in this case Tony Asher claims to have written the whole lyric by himself. Love, meanwhile, claims to have merely added the lines 'Good night baby/sleep tight baby' in the fade (a contribution which most musicians I know would consider an arrangement, rather than songwriting, contribution).

Love nonetheless now has equal co-writing credit, and thanks to the terms of the judgement and of Asher's contract, now gets a greater share of the royalties of this song than does Asher, who wrote the entire lyric.

Before I move on to the other songs, two little anecdotes. Firstly, the first time I saw the touring 'Beach Boys' (Love and Johnston, plus John Cowsill of The Cowsills and various (extremely good) sidemen) was at Warwick Castle in 2001, and it was an open-air gig in some of the worst weather of my life. It was a great gig despite the weather, but it was hardly reminiscent of a California beach.

Then Bruce Johnston announced they were going to play some songs from *Pet Sounds*, the first note of this song was played, and the rain stopped instantly. It remained bright and sunny through this, *Sloop John B* and *God Only Knows*, and through *Good Vibrations*. Then the band started playing *Kokomo* and the heavens opened again. The closest thing I've ever seen to evidence that there is a God .

Secondly, something that has made me unable to listen to this song in quite the same light, a thread on a message board my friend Tilt pointed me to, talking about 'great shootings in rock music' (*I Shot The Sheriff*, that sort of thing), someone replied "the ice cream man at the start of *Wouldn't It Be Nice*". . .

You Still Believe In Me

The backing track for this was recorded before Brian and Asher started working together, and the song was provisionally titled *In My Childhood* (a phrase which fits the first five notes of the intro and also those of the verse melody perfectly), hence the appearance of bicycle bells and horns on the track, which is mostly driven by heavily-reverbed harpsichord and bass guitar.

A more interesting connection to the childhood theme, though, and one which I believe has never been remarked upon, is the horn arrangement. Brian has mentioned that the middle eight to *Wouldn't It Be Nice* is influenced by Glenn Miller (something I can't see myself), and it's well known that the version of *Rhapsody In Blue* he first listened to growing up, which had a huge influence on him, was by the Miller orchestra.

What nobody seems to have remarked on before is that the horn section here is in clear imitation of Miller's style – Miller's sax section was unusual in having a clarinet at the top of a stack of four saxophones. (Normally in swing music the clarinet was a separate lead instrument, as in the Benny Goodman and Artie Shaw bands, or was absent altogether). Here Brian is clearly going for the lush sound of slower Miller pieces like *Moonlight Serenade*, though rather than four saxes and a clarinet he has three saxes, a clarinet and a bass clarinet. The effect – a closely-harmonised block of saxes with a clarinet on top – is still the same, however.

To add to this, these horns come in just before the backing vocals, for four bars, and as soon as the backing vocals come in they all drop out except the clarinet – the most voice-like of the instruments, this stays in as part of the vocal blend. Astonishingly clever stuff. One other thing to note, but which you can't miss, is the way the instrumentation drops down to just a bass 'heartbeat'. This will be another recurring theme throughout this album.

The intro, which was recorded later, is Brian holding the keys down on a piano while Tony Asher plucks the strings inside it, with Brian double-tracked singing the same notes (if you listen closely you can hear that for the last few notes he attempts to harmonise on the lower of the two tracks and fluffs it slightly).

Lyrically, this is all Asher, which is surprising, as it fits precisely the themes that go throughout Wilson's work, of the Goddess-like lover forgiving the imperfect, unworthy man. But Asher and Wilson collaborated so closely at this point that Asher was definitely writing 'as Brian Wilson' rather than as himself – writing lyrics that fit the things Wilson wanted to talk about.

Brian Wilson takes the lead (double-tracked), and Mike Love sings the answering wordless phrase after "I wanna cry".

That's Not Me

The most traditionally 'Beach Boys' sounding track on the album, this is also the only track on which the Beach Boys themselves play – Brian plays organ, Carl guitar and Dennis drums on the basic track, with either Al Jardine or Terry Melcher on tambourine, depending on who you believe. There were only minimal overdubs by session players, and this startlingly empty-sounding track actually points the way forward, more than any other track on *Pet Sounds*, to the organ-dominated sparse productions on *Smiley Smile* and *Friends*, even while pointing backwards to earlier songs, with its Mike lead with Brian singing odd lines (he sings "you needed my love and I know that I left at the wrong time" and "I'm glad I left now I'm that much more sure that we're ready").

Probably the closest thing to filler on the album, this still works thematically and provides a welcome minor respite between the two most emotionally intense pieces on the album.

Don't Talk (Put Your Head On My Shoulder)

A strong contender for one of the most beautiful love songs ever written, attention has often been called – rightly – to the way the bass part and the kettledrums on this both take the role of the heartbeat mentioned in the lyrics. But the real beauty of this song (which features no Beach Boys other than Brian) is in the exquisite chord sequence.

While there are guitars on here (one tremolo one and the other playing a simple answering phrase), what holds the track together is the string sextet (and the organ pad), and that's because the chords here, with their close clustering, and with movement mostly being by single steps in one or two notes of the chords, are perfect for strings.

Listen to the way the chords under the line "I can hear so much in your sighs" slowly open up – we start with E♭m, then add in the seventh. We then move that seventh down to make E♭m6 (minor sixths turn up all over *Pet Sounds*) but now have F# (the minor third) in the bass – the album, again, is full of thirds and fifths in the bass, rather than the conventional root note. And from there we move smoothly to F7, which has the same C and E♭ notes in the chord while the other two notes have moved down a tone and a semitone.

In this sequence we've started with a tight, closed minor chord and ended up with an open, happy major chord with seventh, while never moving more than half the notes in the chord, and never by more than a tone. And we've moved up a tone even though all the individual progressions have been down.

That part is, of course, played on the organ – the strings haven't come in yet at that part – but this sort of thing is tailor-made for creating interesting chord voicings out of interweaving melodies, and that's what Brian does.

The string overdub for this track – which can be heard separately on the *Pet Sounds Sessions* box set – works without any of the rest of the instruments, and is some of the most sophisticated arrangement work I've ever heard in a pop/rock context.

But of course none of that would matter if the melody itself didn't stand up – but it does. As Elvis Costello said (when talking about an album he made in collaboration with opera singer Anne Sofie von Otter, on which she sang this and *You Still Believe In Me)* "Last summer, I heard *Don't Talk (Put Your Head on My Shoulder)* played on the cello. It sounded beautiful and sad, just as it does on *Pet Sounds*. So now you know, if all the record players in the world get broken tomorrow, these songs could be heard a hundred years from now." He's right.

I'm Waiting For The Day

Brian's least favourite song on the album, this was also (on its original release) the only song to credit Mike Love as a co-writer. Originally written in 1964 (when a slightly different version was copyrighted under Brian's name alone), this is the one song on the album that I could imagine writing myself – the chord changes are simplistic, with only the minor sixth in the chorus to give it any real flavour.

Nonetheless, it's a triumph of arrangement – the pounding kettledrum intro (played by Gary Coleman), the flute trio, and the shifts in tempo add a huge amount of interest to an otherwise by-the-numbers song, as does the string interlude which comes out of nowhere before the outro, which sounds like it's wandered in from an altogether better song.

Apparently Brian sings all the parts on this himself, though if he does the bass part is lower than I've ever heard him sing on anything else.

Let's Go Away For A While

A gorgeous instrumental piece of vibraphone-led exotica, inspired by Burt Bacharach, about which I can't find much to say other than that it's beautiful and it fits with the album. One thing I can say though is that I am certain I hear voices singing wordlessly along with the melody on the fade – I'd go so far as to say I can identify one of the voices as Brian's then-wife Marilyn Wilson. There are no vocalists credited, no vocal tracks exist, and I have never seen anyone else mention this, but I swear I can hear it. Am I going mad?[3]

---

[3] After originally posting this essay on my blog, my friend Alex Wilcock informed me that he can hear it too. This suggests that if I am mad, it is at least a *folie a deux*, which is cheering.

Sloop John B

And so after three Brian Wilson solo tracks in a row, at the end of side one we finally get another Beach Boys performance, and a fine one it is too.

Suggested by Al Jardine, the resident folkie of the group, this is a West Indian folk song that had been recorded by, among others, the Weavers and the Kingston Trio. Jardine modified the song slightly (adding in the B♭m chord, for a grand total of four chords) in the expectation that he would get to sing lead.

In fact Brian took Jardine's idea and turned it into a test for the type of production he would use on the *Pet Sounds* album – this song was recorded before much of the rest of the album and was originally intended as a stand-alone single – having the song driven by glockenspiel, flute and twelve-string guitar and writing an ornate vocal arrangement, including the song's *a capella* break, which inspired the Beatles' similar use of the technique in *Paperback Writer*.

While Jardine didn't, as he had assumed, get to sing solo lead, he is one of three lead vocalists here. Brian takes the lead on the first verse, then Brian and Jardine harmonise on the first chorus (Wilson changed the lyric of the song from "I feel so break up" to "I feel so broke up", and you can clearly hear Jardine sing "brea-oke up"), Love takes the second verse ("the first mate he got drunk") and then Brian takes the last verse.

An incredible feat of arrangement and production, and a great single, this ultimately is something of an outlier in the Beach Boys' work – Brian Wilson trying his production techniques on something utterly different from their usual material, rather than being something that fits the rest of the album.

God Only Knows

It's difficult to talk dispassionately about this song as, more than any other track on the album, it's the kind of perfect construction that seems to come as one piece, perfectly formed. Good as, say, *Don't Talk (Put Your Head On My Shoulder)* is, I can imagine writing it myself, were I talented enough. I can look at it afterward and see why Brian made the choices he made, and retrace his steps.

God Only Knows, on the other hand, is not a song that can really be pulled apart and put back together again. Other than the key change for the instrumental break, the song is only twelve bars of actual musical material, repeated in a very simple ballad form, but those twelve bars are just astonishingly beautiful.

In fact, pretty much all the production work on this track seems to have been about stripping it down. The backing track is still full at crucial points, with violin, flute, French horn, harpsichord and accordion at points – but the first verse has only piano, bass, and percussion (provided by Jim Gordon, whose contributions to mid-period Beach Boys records tend to get airbrushed out of history due to his unfortunate later history[4]). This builds during the song, but despite having eighteen different musicians, the song never gets overloaded.

But in order to get that sparse feel, Brian had to try a number of different effects in the studio.

The idea of playing the instrumental bridge staccato came from session pianist Don Randi, the beautiful three-part vocal round at the end was originally sung over a block of 'bop bop bops' sung by the whole band plus Brian's wife and sister-in-law and Terry Melcher, and early mixes

---

[4] Gordon has spent the last three decades in a psychiatric hospital, and thus has been unavailable for the kind of interviews his colleagues regularly give.

feature a godawful sax solo in place of the wordless vocals in the middle.

Lyrically, the song is interesting in that while it starts off very cleverly — "I may not always love you, but..." being one of the more arresting openings of a love song — the sheer force of the obsession in the lyrics comes off as a little creepy. I've seen this referred to as 'the most beautiful suicide song of all time' and while that's not entirely true, it's certainly a self-obsessed song in a way that few of Brian Wilson's are.

The 'you' being sung to is only important insofar as she affects the singer and how the singer affects her. "I may not always love you, but that's OK because I'll just prove that I do and it'll never happen anyway. On the other hand if you ever stop loving me I'll have no reason to live". This is a beautiful song but not, perhaps, an especially healthy one.

Which is why the single best decision Brian made was to have his brother Carl sing this one. While Brian's vocals (audible on earlier mixes on the *Pet Sounds Sessions* box set) work, they have an intensity to them that pushes the song further into creepiness. Carl, on the other hand, sings with an angelic innocence and purity that takes the sting out of the words — the 'if you should ever leave me' becomes as unlikely as the 'I may not always love you', because he's absolutely undisturbed by the line.

This is the vocal with which Carl established himself as the new *de facto* lead singer of the band. The only other vocalists to be featured on the track are Brian and Bruce — on the tag Brian sings both the low and high parts, while Bruce answers him in the same way he did on *California Girls*.

I Know There's An Answer

An odd one out on the album, this song was written by Brian with the band's then road manager, Terry Sachen, and is a hippie berate-everyone-else song in the style that George Harrison would later make his own, though with clunkier lyrics – "I know so many people who think they can do it alone/they isolate their heads and stay in their safety zone" is a bit of a come-down from the careful crafting of Tony Asher's lyrics to the previous song.

Musically simple, this is notable instrumentally mostly for the use of the bass harmonica (which was to inspire its use on various tracks on *Sgt Pepper* the next year) and the banjo (played by Glen Campbell).

Vocally, it's interesting to see just how alike the various Beach Boys could sound – Mike Love takes the first line of each verse, Al Jardine the rest of the verse, and Brian the chorus, yet most people would swear it was a single lead vocalist throughout.

It's also notable for being the cause of one of the biggest arguments the band would have during the making of this album – Mike Love thought the chorus lyrics "Hang on to your ego/Hang on but I know that you're gonna lose the fight" were a reference to the LSD-inspired idea of 'ego death', and insisted on rewriting those lines to "I know there's an answer/I know now but I had to find it by myself", as well as changing "how can I come on when I know I'm guilty?" to "how can I come on and tell them the way that they live could be better?"

Here Today

While Brian was working on this album, he was also working on the single *Good Vibrations*, and several of the Beach Boys have said they think that track should have been included on this album. I disagree – the song wouldn't have fit – but if we had had a hypothetical *Pet Sounds Vibrations* this is what it would have sounded like.

The last collaboration between Wilson and Asher, this is a halfway house between *That's Not Me* and *Good Vibrations*, having a Mike Love lead and being in the keys of A and F#m, like the former, while being created as a patchwork out of ideas that had come up in the GV sessions – it has the same organ-and-plucked-bass verse, the same quiet verses building up to big choruses, and so on. Both start with a change down from a minor chord to a major a tone below, both are built around descending chord sequences.

This sounds very much of a part with the early, R&B-influenced, takes of *Good Vibrations* that were being recorded at that time. There are some nice musical ideas – the descending trombone bassline in the chorus, for example – but this isn't a song anyone involved (except Bruce Johnston) has any especial love for, and it's easy to see why. While a good track – it's easily one of the most commercial things on the album – it's ultimately a piece where its composer took a few experimental ideas and forced them into a conventional shape just to get something done.

The mono mix of this is also famously shoddy, with studio noise leaking all over the instrumental break. This studio noise is actually isolated as a hidden track on one of the discs of the *Pet Sounds Sessions* box set, and consists of some breath noises, some attempts at hitting a falsetto note, Bruce saying "do you have that attached to the flash, do you have it rigged up?", someone (Dennis?) replying "Yeah, I do", Bruce saying "very good" and Brian shouting "top please!" to get the tape rewound. So now you know what that was. These noises aren't on the stereo mix. There are actually more noises under the second verse too, but these have never been isolated like that, officially at least.

One of the only two songs on the album with a Mike lead vocal, this is also one of the most "Beach Boys" sounding tracks, to the extent that the current touring "Beach Boys" occasionally perform it live very creditably – though oddly Bruce takes lead on the lines starting on a D chord (e.g. "A brand new love affair is such a beautiful thing", the first half of the bridges).

I Just Wasn't Made For These Times

Possibly the most 'Brian' song on the album, while Tony Asher wrote the lyrics for this he's stated many times that he was pretty much taking dictation, and has never really 'got' the emotions behind it. Singing in a low register where he sounds at times uncannily like his brother Dennis (listen especially to his pronunciation of the word 'found' in the second verse, and compare to Dennis' vocals on the very similar *In The Back Of My Mind*), the sentiments here are perhaps a little jejune, but nonetheless from the heart, and this song had a huge impact on me when I was sixteen.

The line "they say I got brains, but they ain't doing me no good/I wish they could" probably did more to make me a Beach Boys fan than any other moment in the band's career, and for all that it's easy to mock that as the kind of thing every 'sensitive' teenager ever has thought, 'sensitive' teenagers need music too.

However, for a song whose sentiments basically boil down to "nobody likes me, everybody hates me, think I'll go eat worms", the music really is exquisitely constructed. Like much of *Pet Sounds* there's no drum kit until the chorus, the song being driven by harpsichord and bass in the verses and Frank Capp's clip-clop percussion in the bridges, with Hal Blaine adding punctuating kettledrums in the second verse.

And in the choruses we have a wonderfully bizarre mix of instruments – Blaine's drum kit being almost clodhopping in its straightforwardness, while Don Randi's barrelhouse piano, way down in the mix, chases the percussion around like a soundtrack to a silent comedy, before breaking down into a heartbreaking little melodic fragment played simultaneously on tenor sax and theremin (actually an electro-theremin, an instrument invented by session player Paul Tanner, that sounded like a theremin but was easier to play accurately).

To my ears, Brian is the only Beach Boy on the track, but there's a whole stack of Brians.

On the chorus we have three of him singing "O cuando sere, un dia sere" (Spanish for "when will I be, one day I will be"), while at each repetition is introduced a further Brian with a further repeated line – one singing "sometimes I feel very sad", one singing "Ain't found the right thing to put my heart and soul into" a little higher, and finally, so high he's almost screaming, one singing "People I know don't wanna be where I'm at". A gorgeous song, however immature the sentiment.

Pet Sounds

An exotica-flavoured track, this owes equally to three separate influences. Most obviously there's Jack Nitzsche's surf instrumentals, like *The Lonely Surfer* or *Surf Finger*, which share the clip-clopping feel and reverbed Fender guitar. (So close are the similarities that when REM recorded their tribute to Nitzsche, *2JN*, it came out sounding far more like this track than any of Nitzsche's...)

Second there's the exotica of Martin Denny and Les Baxter, with the reverbed percussion and mildly dissonant horns.

And finally there's John Barry's work on the James Bond scores (this track was originally titled "Run, James, Run", and was half-intended to be submitted to the Bond film producers), particularly the way Barry's arrangement of Monty Norman's *James Bond Theme* had the melody played on electric guitar over a repetitive vamp. The whole thing adds up to a minor track, but a pleasant rest between two of the most emotionally intense tracks on the album.

Caroline, No

The final track on the album is almost a musical rewrite of *Don't Talk*, having the same feel and many of the same chord relations and voicings (the Fm7/A♭ – E♭m7/D♭ change under the verses here being very similar to the D♭7-Am♭7 changes in the choruses to the earlier song). However, where there the music had been in the service of a feeling of comfort and love, here it is in the service of a song about hurt, and lost innocence (this song's similarity to *Wonderful* from the next album has never, in my view, been adequately explored).

Originally titled "Oh Carol, I Know", the more negative title came from Brian mishearing Tony Asher, and it's a shame, because the earlier title is less judgemental than this one. However, this did lead to the rather smart wordplay in the second verse, where instead of "Oh Caroline No" he sings "Oh Caroline you" (oh Carol, I knew).

This was originally recorded a semitone slower, and was sped up on the advice of Brian's father, Murry Wilson, 'to make him sound younger'. One of the few decent bits of advice Murry ever gave, this stopped the track from feeling quite so dirge-like, and made it a fitting close to the album. Outside that context, it was released as a solo single for Brian and made the lower reaches of the US Top 40.

From its opening percussion (played on water bottles) to the closing sound of a train being barked at by two dogs (Brian's dogs Banana and Louie) the whole song has a melancholy air that is the absolute antithesis of the album's hopeful opening. But you can always turn the album over and start again. Maybe next time it'll end differently…

Bonus track

Various bonus tracks, usually alternate versions of tracks on the album, have been issued on the different CD issues of this album, but one that is there consistently is *Trombone Dixie*. An instrumental that was never released at the time, and recorded around the start of sessions for the album, it's pleasant enough, bearing a strong resemblance both to *Wouldn't It Be Nice* and especially to the late-1965 single *The Little Girl I Once Knew*, and having some ideas that Brian would come back to for *Holidays* on *Smile*. But it's a minor work and it's easy to see why it was left off the finished album.

Good Vibrations

While for the most part I am dealing with the Beach Boys' music on an album-by-album basis, with this song (and one other I shall get to in volume two) it feels wrong. The album this was eventually released on, *Smiley Smile*, is to my mind possibly the best the band released, yet this track still sits in the middle like a black hole, distorting the feel of the whole album in a profound way.

I have sixty-five different versions of this song in my MP3/FLAC collection, not counting copies on vinyl or CD. The worst is a version by Mike Love and Adrian Baker from the 1980s, the best is the version that was released as a single. For all the live performances, outtakes, covers and alternative versions, nobody has ever beaten the three minutes and thirty-nine seconds of mono glory that came out on October 10, 1966. It may well be the greatest pop single ever released by anyone.

It was certainly the height of the Beach Boys' commercial and artistic success – it was their first UK number one, but their last (for 22 years, at any rate) in the USA. It took just over five months' work, from the recording of the basic backing track on February 17th 1966, to the final electro-theremin overdub on 21 September, to create the track. At least two sets of lyrics were written for it, and it spanned the recording of two different albums before being released on a third.

That original, February 17, session has been released in part in various places, most recently on the *Good Vibrations* 40th Anniversary Single, where it's the beginning part of what's credited as *Good Vibrations (various sessions)*. You can hear, listening through these session recordings, that the basic verse/chorus of the song was there from the very beginning, but that the rest of the structure took a lot of tinkering and experimentation. Many of the ideas that were thrown out during these sessions (such as the 'hum-de-ah' vocal parts) would have been the principal hook for any other band.

We can hear the original conception of the song most clearly on the alternate version released as a bonus track on the *Smiley Smile/Wild Honey* CD, which is the 17th February backing track with a guide vocal put on by Brian the next day.

Listening to it, Brian originally intended the track to be a 'psychedelic R&B' track, and already has the verse and chorus music worked out. What we have here, in fact, is very closely related to several *Pet Sounds* tracks – the arrangement and general feel are similar to that of *Here Today*, the electro-theremin part is similar to that of *I Just Wasn't Made For These Times*, while the melody is a cousin of *God Only Knows*. In fact, the best way of thinking about this track is that it's taken the lowest common denominator of *Here Today* and *God Only Knows* and turned the result into an R&B track. We have the same minor-third key change between verse and chorus we've seen throughout *Pet Sounds*, the same descending scalar chord sequences, the same mobile bass parts, but here, rather than to express melancholy, these things are used in a way that's as close as Brian Wilson ever got to funky.

However, after those first two verse/choruses, Brian seems to run out of ideas, and much of the rest of the track is more or less vamping. Tony Asher's lyric, too, is half-formed. The idea's there – the basic concept of a man 'picking up' 'good vibrations' from a woman (which came from Brian's own thoughts about telepathy), but it's clearly a dummy lyric:

> She's already working on my brain
>
> I only look in her eyes
>
> But I pick up something I just can't explain
>
> I pick up good, good, good, good vibrations, yeah
>
> I bet I know what she's like
>
> And I can feel how right/good she'd be for me
> *Brian sings both words on this double-tracked vocal*
>
> It's weird how she comes in so strong
>
> And I wonder what she's picking up from me
>
> I hope it's good, good, good, good vibrations, yeah

The result is close enough to the finished version that you can see where he's going, but at this point it would have been an album track at best.

Fast forward five months and what we have is something very different. Firstly, we have new lyrics by Mike Love. I'm not normally a huge fan of Love's lyrics, but this time he's done something quite clever:

> I, I love the colourful clothes she wears,
>
> And the way the sunlight plays upon her hair
>
> I hear the sound of a gentle word
>
> On the wind that lifts her perfume through the air

> I'm picking up good vibrations
>
> She's giving me excitations

Whereas Asher's original lyric had focused solely on the extra-sensory aspects ("She's already working on my brain" "I pick up something I just can't explain"), Love here grounds the song in the sensual and earthy before the more ethereal lyrics of the chorus. Note how he manages to work in sight (the colourful clothes, the sunlight), hearing (the sound of the gentle word) and smell (the perfume).

This gives the song a grounding in the earthy, the quotidian, which allows the lyric to take the listener into more outrageous places and be sure the listener will follow. Whereas Asher's lyric alienates, Love's lyric draws us in.

The other major change suggested by Love is, of course, the good vibrations/excitations lyric. This is exactly the kind of dumb-but-brilliant idea Love was so good at, at his best. Taking the fairly low-profile bass part and turning it into a hook was a stroke of genius.

The finished recording is a patchwork, but somehow manages to be amazingly coherent. Let's go through the different sections and see what's going on.

We start with the sixteen-bar first verse I quote above. Coming straight in on the first word with no intro, we have Carl singing over just organ (played by Larry Knechtel) and bass (presumably either Carol Kaye or Ray Pohlman – I can't find a copy of the session logs for the Feb 17 session, and so am going by the logs from April 9 onwards[5]) this verse recording sounds to me in fact like it comes from that very first session. Flute (Jay Migliori) and drums and percussion (Jim Gordon and Hal Blaine) come in on bar

---

[5] Available at http://www.angelfire.com/mn/smileshop/sessionlogs.html , the relevant sessions are those for *Good Vibrations* and for the working title *Inspiration*.

nine, which also helps to disguise one of the more interesting edits on the record.

Listen again to that line "I hear the sound of a gentle word" and you can tell it isn't just Carl singing. The first half of the line – "I hear the sound of a" is in fact Brian, sounding a lot like Carl but clearly more nasal and less breathy (in fact it may be Brian doubling Carl. There are two voices there with different timbres – one may be Carl, but the more prominent is definitely Brian). The same thing happens on the line "when I look in her eyes" in the second verse.

This is an odd decision to make, frankly, as Carl could hit those notes (although they were to the top of his range). One can only presume that he just had difficulty with them – this being, after all, only his fourth real lead vocal. Listening to concert recordings, Carl would be doubled by someone (I think Bruce) on very early live versions of this song (e.g. the Michigan performance on the *Good Vibrations: Thirty Years Of the Beach Boys* box set) but by late 1967 (e.g. the 'concert rehearsal' take on the *Endless Harmony* rarities collection) Carl was singing the line solo.

Either way, it's something that, once you've noticed it, you can't unnotice, but manages to escape most people's attention...

Harmonically, this section is just a scalar descending pattern in E♭m, going down from the tonic to the dominant twice, before the second time it goes into the subtonic leading into the chorus.

The chorus starts with Mike Love singing, solo, the line "I'm picking up good vibrations/she's giving me excitations" over a two-chord shuffle in F#. This two-chord vamp seems to come from *Can I Get A Witness* by way of the Ad-Libs' *The Boy From New York City* (both of which are songs the Beach Boys had referenced before, on *Carl's Big Chance* and *The Girl From New York City*), and this is obvious in the basic backing track, but the jazz-tinged bassline/vocal part disguises this somewhat, and the cellos playing triplets (a suggestion of Carl Wilson) make the resemblance seem distant. But listen to *Can I Get A Witness* and you'll see you can sing this line over the top easily. However between the cello part and the electro-theremin (played by Paul Tanner) this sounds like nothing else on Earth.

(Well, almost nothing — it's been suggested that this section of the song bears more than a slight resemblance to Delia Derbyshire's realisation of Ron Grainer's *Doctor Who* theme. According to Lawrence Miles and Tat Wood's *About Time* series of Doctor Who guidebooks, Carl Wilson used to watch the show in his dressing room before gigs in the UK. However, looking at the dates, prior to the recording of *Good Vibrations* the band had only been in the UK for one broadcast of Doctor Who — *Planet Of Giants* episode two — and they were on BBC TV themselves that day, though I've been unable to find out precisely what time, so it seems extraordinarily unlikely that any of them had ever seen the show, still less seen it often enough to remember the theme tune).

We then repeat this line, but with a three part harmony (sounding to me like Brian, Carl and Al) girl-group answering phrase ("ooh bop bop, good vibrations, bop bop excitations").

We then depart from the original February version — the whole thing then moves a tone up, and we add another, falsetto, Brian singing "good, good, good, good vibrations, ah". This falsetto Brian part is actually the original chorus melody, but here it's just a final element in an intricate tapestry of music and vocals. We then move another tone up and repeat this last line. This movement of a two-chord chorus vamp up in stages of a tone at a time is something that Brian is reusing from *California Girls*.

There's then a hard edit into the second verse on the last "excitations", and we repeat the verse and chorus musical material almost exactly, but at the end of the second verse we go into a completely different section.

We start with a continuation of the ending chorus vamp between B♭ and E♭/B♭, but this time played on tack piano (Al de Lory), bass and jew's harp (Tommy Morgan), with 'ah' vocals and flute (piccolo?) coming in part way through. We briefly move to vamping between B♭ and A♭ for Mike's "I don't know where but she sends me there" and Brian's "Oh my my what a sensation", before returning to the original vamp for Mike's answering "Oh my my what an elation". All this material is still based on the chorus, but sounds stunningly different.

We then have a simple, almost churchlike, three-chord section in F, with Dennis playing the organ, hand percussion (Blaine?) and piccolo. This starts out instrumental, and then Mike comes in with "Gotta keep those lovin' good vibrations happening with her". After this line, the bass comes in, and Brian sings the same line in falsetto, harmonising with Mike. They sing the line again, but their vocals fade out, replaced by Tommy Morgan's harmonica, which continues playing the same phrase until the held F chord and "ah" vocal from the entire band.

There follows a brief reprise of the chorus material, but this time instead of going up in whole tones, it moves rapidly downward, ending up on B.

We then have a single, pulsing, bass note under a falsetto "na na na na na, na na na" (which actually doesn't sound like Brian's falsetto to me, strangely enough – I suspect this is actually sped up, and may be Carl or Al). We move up a tone, continuing this falsetto melody while Mike answers underneath with "ba ba ba ba ba, ba", move up a tone again and have someone in the middle (Carl?) singing "do do do, do do, do do", move back down a tone continuing this (note the constant obsession with wholetone movements here), before suddenly everything drops out the cello and electro-theremin come in, and they repeat the chorus riff to fade, with the other instruments coming in, staying in the key of A♭ (the same key as the third line of the chorus).

That's, by my count, at least seven distinct sections in this three and a half minutes of music, all variations of at least one of two ideas – whole tone steps and two-chord shuffles.

As a song, *Good Vibrations* barely exists – it's not something you can sit down with an acoustic guitar or piano and play and expect it to sound particularly good – it's something rather different, a play with theme and variations in a way one doesn't normally get in pop music, an experiment in production, the combination of instruments, and the use of the studio to create sounds one could never otherwise hear. Everything is hammering home the idea of 'vibrations' – the church organ, the jittery triplet cellos, the ethereal electro-theremin, all sounding spectacularly different from almost anything.

Nothing like this had ever been recorded before, or ever would again.

line-up

Brian Wilson, Carl Wilson, Dennis Wilson, Mike Love, Al Jardine, Bruce Johnston

Smiley Smile/Wild Honey

1967 was in many ways the most important turning point in the Beach Boys' career. After *Pet Sounds,* the musical world was waiting on tenterhooks for the next Beach Boys album, *Smile*, a collaboration between Brian Wilson and Van Dyke Parks that would, according to Dennis Wilson, 'make *Pet Sounds* stink'.

Due to a combination of intra-band tensions, legal problems between the band and Capitol records, and Brian Wilson's worsening mental health, the album was never finished, though most of it has surfaced over the years on compilations, and Brian Wilson made a re-recorded, complete, version in 2004, with Parks' assistance.[6]

Instead, the band regrouped - initially without Johnston, who was disaffected enough to leave the band for a few months, and recorded a new album, *Smiley Smile*, based on the *Smile* material but featuring mostly just the Beach Boys themselves instrumentally.

This stripped-down, almost amateurish, sound, which continued in various forms for the two albums after this, was a critical and commercial flop. Where listeners had been promised a progressive, psychedelic masterpiece, they got stoned giggling, songs about vegetables, and some-

---

[6]For more on *Smile*, see vol 2 of this book, where we will deal with the *Good Vibrations* box set and the (as of this writing) forthcoming 2001 *Smile Sessions* release, and vol 3, which will look at Brian Wilson's solo re-recording.

thing that sounded small and intimate at a time when everyone was expecting bigger, more flamboyant, recordings.

However, with the benefit of hindsight, these albums contain some of the band's very best work.

Smiley Smile

Smiley Smile shares two things in common with *The Beach Boys Love You*, an album that came out ten years later - they are the only two Beach Boys albums to consist entirely of previously-unreleased Brian Wilson songs, and they are the two albums which most polarise Beach Boys fandom.

In general, the split for both is along age-related lines. Those under about forty-five, whose musical tastes were influenced by punk and post-punk indie music, tend to love both albums, and think of them as examples of raw, unvarnished genius. Those older than that see them as embarrassing, shambolic messes. (There are, of course, exceptions on both sides).

I am thirty-two, and *Smiley Smile* and *Love You* are my two favourite Beach Boys albums.

Recorded almost entirely in Brian Wilson's home studio, *Smiley Smile* is an astonishingly fragile, beautiful album, unlike anything I've ever heard in the history of popular music. Over extraordinarily bare instrumental tracks - often just a single Baldwin organ or one-note piano or bass part, with ambient noises and stoned laughter, and with a certain amount of studio trickery (mostly playing with tape speed), we have fragile, whimsical, half-thought-out but gorgeous melodies, sung with some of the greatest vocal performances of all time.

It's minimalist, beautiful, fragile, gorgeous, at times hilariously funny, at times impenetrable. Although it was released as much through desperation as anything else, it's probably the bravest album ever released by a major artist - the sudden shifts in style of a Dylan or Bowie are nothing compared to this.

This was also the first Beach Boys album to feature Carl Wilson's voice more prominently than any other, and the first to have a credit of 'produced by the Beach Boys' rather than 'produced by Brian Wilson'. Both of these are signs of things to come.

line-up

Brian Wilson, Carl Wilson, Dennis Wilson, Mike Love, Al Jardine, Bruce Johnston (tracks one, two and six only)

Heroes & Villains

According to legend (and where *Smile* is concerned there's more legend than fact), on the first day Brian Wilson and Van Dyke Parks collaborated, they wrote four songs - *Heroes & Villains*, *Wonderful*, *Cabinessence* and *Surf's Up*. If true, this may well have been the most productive day's work in history - at least two of those four songs have a reasonable claim for the title of 'greatest song ever written'.

Whether true or not, it is known that this song definitely was the first collaboration between the two, and it was to have been the centrepiece of the *Smile* album - its themes both lyrical (growing old and looking back at youth and forward to the youth of the next generation, the Old West, escape) and musical (the chorus theme recurs in the majority of the *Smile* music) would have tied the album together. And the song went through a huge number of reworkings in the studio, with many sections being recorded and discarded.

The version that was finally released as a single, consisting mostly of *Smile* recordings, is a masterpiece, though a more intellectual one than the Beach Boys' earlier works - whereas Brian and his previous collaborators are or were primarily concerned with evoking emotion, Parks at this point was more interested in exploring ideas.

Starting off over a track based very closely on Phil Spector's production of *Save The Last Dance For Me* for Ike and Tina Turner, the melody and chord sequence of the first two verses are almost moronically simple - a simple stepwise descent (scales, especially descending ones, show up over and over again in *Smile*) over a chord sequence of I, V-of-V and V.

But while Brian had obviously been thinking of Phil Spector when writing the music, Parks had been thinking of Marty Robbins and Western ballads, and so we have a torrent of punning syllables telling a story of the old west:

> I've been in this town so long that back in the city I've been taken for lost and gone and unknown for a long, long time
>
> Fell in love years ago with an innocent girl from the Spanish and Indian home of the heroes and villains
>
> Once at night cotillion squared the fight and she was right in the rain of the bullets that eventually brought her down
>
> But she's still dancing in the night unafraid of what a dude'll do in the town full of heroes and villains

Clever as it seems, some of this lyric loses a great deal

out of the larger context of the *Smile* album - the 'dude'll do' for example is meant to reference a cock crow, which would tie in to the song *Barnyard* ("Out in the barnyard, the chickens do their number"), and dancing, American Indians, and facing one's fear would all recur in many of the other songs.

Brian sings these lines over a thumping bass and drum track with the rest of the band providing simple 'ooh' harmonies in the first verse, growing steadily more complex and contrapuntal before we go into the chorus.

The chorus to *Heroes & Villains* is yet another example of the musical idea that had been obsessing Brian for the previous two years and that dominated the unreleased *Smile* - a two-chord riff (similar intervals to the *Good Vibrations* chorus, but a tone lower, and with the first chord in the riff being minor rather than major) repeated, which then moves up a whole tone (as in both *Good Vibrations* and *California Girls*). In many ways this chorus can be seen as the culmination of the previous two years' work.

But whereas those songs had intricate, multi-layered orchestrations, the instrumentation on the chorus here is just a harpsichord playing a repeated figure, a Baldwin organ holding down a single note, and some hand percussion. Everything else on this astonishing section of music is the Beach Boys' voices, and the fact that the track can sound so full with so little instrumentation shows how utterly unique they were as a vocal group - something that shines through throughout this album.

We then have a reprise of the verse material, largely wordless, before a fully *a capella* verse which again shows just how far the band had come vocally even in a year - compare the intricate, shimmering, layered contrapuntal motion here to the simple lines of, say, *Sloop John B* .

The next section, featuring vocals, Baldwin and harpsichord again ("my children were raised") has the same melody as the verses, but a totally different chord sequence, the top of the chord (the 'right hand') alternating between C# and F# (the same kind of two-chord shuffle as in the *Good Vibrations* chorus) but with a bassline going up and down an ascending scale from C# to G# and back again. While they don't sound similar, rehearsal takes of this sequence show that it was clearly inspired by *Mister Sandman* by the Chordettes. (For those who are wondering, the backing vocals under this section are singing "boys and girls and boys and girls and...")

And we finish with an *a capella* verse - the melody remaining the same but harmonised much more richly - followed by the chorus to fade.

While one of the best singles the band had ever released to this point, this 'only' reached number 12 in the US chart when it was released, and to all intents and purposes this is the song that marks the end of the Beach Boys as a commercial force in their own country.

Vegetables

This second Wilson/Parks collaboration couldn't be more different - partly because some of Parks' more idiosyncratic original lyrics weren't used.

Over a backing track of just a bass, a blown jug, some sound effects and percussion created by crunching on vegetables, the band sing in unison a simple song about the joys of eating one's greens. Then, at the end, we segue into a recording of the song from the *Smile* sessions - a cascade of overlapping vocals over just a piano (though again, it sounds far, far fuller than that), with Brian singing "I know that you'll feel better when you send us in a letter and tell us the name of your favourite vegetable".

This is so unlike everything else released at the time (though lyrically surprisingly similar to Frank Zappa's roughly contemporaneous *Call Any Vegetable*) that it's unsurprising that listeners turned away in droves. Listening now, though, it still sounds fresh and interesting in a way that much of the more critically-acclaimed music of the time doesn't.

Fall Breaks And Back To Winter (Woody Woodpecker Symphony)

A reworking of an instrumental recorded for *Smile*, *Mrs O'Leary's Cow* (sometimes known as *Fire*) , whereas that track was full of *sturm und drang*, this is gentle and contemplative. Staying for the most part on one chord, we have some absurdly low organ bass going up and down a chromatic scale, while the band sing block-harmony 'aahs'. There's a feeling of nature about the track - what sounds like a harmonica playing excerpts from the Woody Woodpecker theme, and percussion sounding like a woodpecker's beak on wood, while the bass vocals (presumably by Love, though with the tape slowed down) are reminiscent of a bullfrog.

She's Goin' Bald

Credited to Wilson/Love/Parks , Van Dyke Parks' credit is because the earlier part of this song is based on a *Smile* track, *He Gives Speeches*, for which Parks wrote the lyrics. This is actually a wonderfully bizarre Wilson/Love comedy song.

Over a three-chord sequence (I-ii-V7 in F) played on organ and bongos, the band sing a backing vocal part originally written for an unused section of *Heroes and Villains*, while Brian (with Mike answering him) tells a story of peeking in to the room of a woman whose hair is falling out.

(Shades of Swift's *The Lady's Dressing Room* here). Quite why Love found this a laughing matter given that his own hairline was rapidly receding I don't know.

We then have a section with a huge amount of tape speed-up - to the point that the band sound like they're singing through helium - where to the tune of *Get A Job* by the Silhouettes, the band sing "what a blow" (apparently as a play on words - "blow" "job").

Then, in a manner similar to the introductory narration of 1940s radio adventure serials or children's adventure cartoons, we have a description of the woman's actions "she made a bee-line to her room and grabbed all kinda juice/she started pouring it on her head and thought she'd grow it back") over diminished chords on the piano, rising in a chromatic scale from Edim to Bdim.

And we end with a bluesy variant of the original three chord sequence (I7-II7-V in B♭), played on piano, bass and acoustic guitar (the first guitar to appear on this album) as the band sing "you're too late, mama, ain't nothin' upside your head". They're all heart.

Little Pad

A gorgeous little song by Brian with almost no lyrics, this starts with the band giggling and singing the song in comedy voices, before breaking into some gorgeous hummed harmonies with Hawaiian guitar. We then alternate between Carl, backed by guitar, singing wordlessly, Carl backed by organ and clip-clop percussion singing single lines about wanting "a little pad in Hawaii", and the band backed by piano and guitar humming.

The song's a nothing, but it's a gentle, heartfelt, beautiful vocal performance.

Good Vibrations

See separate entry

With Me Tonight

And here, for the first time since *Summer Days*, we have the return of the *Fannie Mae* riff. The song alternates between the band singing "on and on she go down be doo dah" to the same tune as, for example, "help me Rhonda, help help me Rhonda", and wordlessly backing Carl as he sings "with me tonight, I know you're with me tonight".

Rather than being a fully constructed song, this is one of many little fragments of indescribable beauty scattered throughout the album. With just an organ, a bass and his family's voices, Brian Wilson could conjure heart-stopping wonder out of the simplest ingredients.

Wind Chimes

Another utterly strange track that defies analysis in any conventional sense, this is one of the most beautifully strange pieces of music the band ever committed to vinyl. A Wilson/Parks song originally intended for *Smile*, the *Smile* version is a fairly standard pop song in structure, with a steady beat.

The *Smiley Smile* version, though, does everything in its power to get rid of the standard pulse of pop music. While it's still (more or less) keeping to a regular beat, the backing track is just held chords on piano and organ, the titular wind chimes themselves, and free-tempo guitar, and the vocals (shared between Brian, Carl, Dennis and Mike) are sung in a free, off-tempo manner. The whole thing conspires to give the impression of random beauty, while not having a note out of place.

And then, just as the song ends, we have so far down in the mix it's almost inaudible without turning the volume up all the way, one of the most glorious pieces of music in the band's career - the band singing, as a round, the phrase "whispering winds set my wind chimes a tinklin'". Exquisite.

Gettin' Hungry

A Wilson/Love song, this one points the way forward to the R&B flavour of the *Wild Honey* album, but this kind of simplistic rock song doesn't really work in the stripped-down *Smiley Smile* style, and it's the one truly weak track on the album.

Someone must have disagreed, though, because the truly bizarre decision was made to release this as a single - and not even under the Beach Boys' name but as by Brian Wilson and Mike Love. Unsurprisingly, it wasn't a hit.

Love seems to have had a soft spot for the song, though, as he remade it in the late 70s with his side-project, Celebration.

Wonderful

Quite possibly the single most beautiful song ever written, *Wonderful* is another Wilson/Parks song, telling the story of a young girl who goes off and loses her virginity, and her innocence more generally, at a young age:

> Farther down the path was a mystery,
>
> Through the recess, the chalk and numbers
>
> A boy bumped into her one, one, wonderful

before returning, older and wiser, to her parents:

> She'll return, in love with her liberty,
>
> Never known as a non-believer
>
> She'll smile and thank God for one, one, wonderful

In many ways, this can be seen as a counterpart both of *Caroline, No* and of the Beatles' *She's Leaving Home*, but where those songs are judgemental either of the girl or of the parents, this song seeks reconciliation and forgiveness on both sides and suggests that innocence can actually be regained with experience. It's a more mature, reflective song than the other two, great as they undoubtedly are.

Not only that, it manages this while having concern for the aesthetics of the lyric in a way that neither of those other songs do. Both the other songs treat words functionally, as a means of conveying a single piece of information. By contrast, Parks' lyrics are carefully chosen to be beautiful themselves, independent of the meaning they carry. At this point Parks was almost certainly the most artistically advanced lyricist in the music industry.

And the music matches this. A variant of the *Heroes & Villains* melody, this relationship is far less audible on the *Smiley Smile* version than on the version recorded for *Smile*, thanks to the lack of backing vocals, but harmonically this is far closer to pieces like *Caroline, No* or *Don't Talk (Put Your Head On My Shoulder)* than the harmonically simplistic material elsewhere on the album, with a chord change almost every beat.

Carl Wilson's soft, beautiful vocal performance over a piano and organ is suddenly interrupted straight after the 'boy bumping' by a totally different piece of music. Here we have the sounds of a rather stoned party, with people saying things like "don't think you're God... vibrations" while Mike Love sings a lounge singer version of the Heroes & Villains melody over a piano, before we return to the main song. Often dismissed as an unwanted interruption, this new section actually manages to dramatise the situation surrounding our protagonist's loss of innocence well.

If there were any justice in the world, this song would now be regarded as every bit the classic that *God Only Knows* is, as on every level that matters - musical and lyrical sophistication, beauty, the compassion that pours out of every syllable of the song - this is the superior of that song and almost every other I've heard.

Whistle In

And the album finishes with another simple, fragmentary vocal chant, written by Brian most notable for Mike's bass vocal part.

Wild Honey

Whereas *Smiley Smile* had been an act of desperation, on *Wild Honey*, the band seem to have deliberately chosen to keep the stripped-down aesthetic they'd started on the previous album, but to turn it towards more conventional R&B-flavoured rock/pop music.

While it's a less challenging listen than *Smiley Smile*, it also sounds like it was less challenging to record. While it has its moments, it's the first Beach Boys album about which there's nothing innovative, nothing new. Parts of it are half-arsed at best, and there's a distinct feeling of "will this do?" hanging over all but a handful of the best tracks.

This is hardly surprising - Brian Wilson was starting his long process of withdrawal from the band in the wake of the *Smile* disaster, and the rest of the band weren't yet ready to fill his shoes. While all but two of these songs are Wilson/Love collaborations, Carl Wilson's description of this as "a very un-Brian album" is largely true.

Possibly this was understandable. In total this was the sixteenth album the band released in a little over five years. 1967 was to be the last year in which the band would release multiple studio albums, and the music improved because of it.

line-up

Brian Wilson, Carl Wilson, Dennis Wilson, Mike Love, Al Jardine, Bruce Johnston

Wild Honey

The album starts out strong with this great rocker, showcasing a soulful side of Carl Wilson's voice that hadn't been heard before (when I've played this track to people who aren't familiar with it, nobody has guessed it's a Beach Boys track - some have even guessed it's Jack White singing). Based around a simple chord sequence (slightly similar to the other great Beach Boys attempt at R&B, *Sail On, Sailor*), with a piano vamp and an electro-theremin part by Paul Tanner, this should have been a massive hit.

And had it been released a few months later, when every band was going 'back to its roots' and 50s nostalgia was starting to come in, it would have been. In the context of spring 1968, with *Lady Madonna* in the charts, Bill Haley charting again in the UK, and Elvis back on form with *Guitar Man* and *U.S. Male*, this would have made perfect sense. In October 1967, though, with *San Francisco (Flowers In Your Hair)*, and *King Midas In Reverse* in the charts, this sounded like yesterday, not tomorrow, and accordingly only reached number thirty-one in the US and twenty-nine in the UK.

Aren't You Glad

A rather lovely little poppy track that remained in the band's setlist for a couple of years, this song, with its 6th chords, is the most harmonically interesting of the new songs on the album (though that's not saying much). The lead vocal is shared between Mike, Brian and Carl.

Love's verse vocal is one of his very best - he's high in his tenor range here, but singing with hardly a hint of the nasality that usually plagues him in this range, and comfortably bouncing along on top of the music with a light touch he normally doesn't have. And the two Carls on the chorus again show his newfound soul vocal skills.

On the other hand, on the bridge Brian is sounding notably thinner than he had even a year or so earlier, and seems to be straining for notes he would previously have reached with ease. It might be apathy, or it might be the first sign of the slow vocal deterioration that would set in rapidly by the mid-70s, but appears to have slowly started earlier.

I Was Made To Love Her

A creditable cover of Stevie Wonder's then-current hit, this version cuts out the rather jarring "through thick and thin" section from the original (the band recorded this section too, but discarded it), and misses out Wonder's harmonica part. This version swaps the original's light fluidity for something a little heavier and clunkier (the bass on the track is clearly inferior to James Jamerson's wonderful playing, so they've sensibly gone for power over finesse) but also showcases Carl Wilson's talents as a vocal chameleon - his performance here sounds eerily like Wonder.

Country Air

The most *Smiley Smile*-esque of the tracks here, this is another one backed by organ and piano (though this time also with bass and drums) and alternating between wordless vocals and simple, repetitive lyrics chanted by the group. Melodically a rewrite of *Da Doo Ron Ron*, this is a far gentler, softer thing than that record, with a lovely falsetto flourish at the end of each chorus.

A Thing Or Two

I think it says everything that needs to be said about this song that I've listened to this album maybe once a month on average since I bought it sixteen years ago, meaning I must have heard this song a minimum two hundred times, yet when I looked through the tracklist I thought "which one's that again?"

To all intents and purposes a rewrite of *Gettin' Hungry*, it's a more coherent, but more banal, performance and arrangement than that track, though Love and Carl Wilson do their best with the material.

Darlin'

A rewrite of *Thinkin' 'Bout You, Baby*, a song Brian and Mike had written for singer Sharon Marie some three years earlier, the astonishing thing about this is how well the same (or similar) musical material works both at expressing wistful longing in the original and lustful joy in this new version.

Originally offered by Brian to Redwood, the band that later became Three Dog Night, this is a joyous uptempo rocker whose augmented chords and major sevenths make it more harmonically sophisticated than the material around it, and it's a production which has had some attention paid to it, again unlike the surrounding songs. Unfortunately the lyrics haven't had quite the same attention paid to them - "I'm gonna love you every single night, because I think that you're doggone outtasight" is a hard line to sing with any conviction. Fortunately, Carl Wilson more than manages.

Released as a single, this just scraped the top twenty in the US and reached number 11 in the UK. It remains in the setlist of the Beach Boys (and the members' various post-1998 projects) to this day, being one of their best-loved late-60s singles.

I'd Love Just Once To See You

While this song is credited to Wilson/Love, I suspect it was just agreed to give both men joint credit for every song on the album, because this is as obvious an example of a Brian Wilson solo composition as I've ever heard.

This is the first of a series of slice-of-life songs that would become a minor thread running through the next few years of Brian's work, where he would write a song that just described whatever he was thinking or doing at the time. Often these would be some of the best things he would produce.

This isn't one of his best songs, but it is a fun, light song that manages to overcome its obviously impromptu nature by virtue of its childlike lightness of touch and honesty. And the punchline to the song is genuinely funny the first time you hear it.

Brian sings lead here, and sounds more engaged than on anything else on the album. He's occasionally performed this live (notably on the *Smile* tours in 2004).

Here Comes The Night

Another Brian lead, and we're back to the organ-led R&B feel again. Not the Them song of the same name, this is a rather by-the-numbers song which however manages the interesting trick of having the chorus apparently lose its tonal centre altogether - normally one would have a harmonically simple chorus while the verses are complex, but this has simple verses in C but a chorus whose chords are Cmin, A♭7 and F, which are chords that just should not go together.

Not one of the better songs on the album, this was nonetheless liked enough by the band that they remade it twelve years later in an ill-advised attempt to 'go disco'.

Let The Wind Blow

A Wilson/Love song, apparently more by Love than Wilson, this is rightly regarded as a classic. Harmonically simplistic, this has a gorgeous melody which does have more of Love's fingerprints than Wilson's on it (compare to, say, *Big Sur* from the *Holland* album). The 'arched' backing vocals, going up and down the scale wordlessly, are definitely Wilson's contribution, though, bearing a strong resemblance to motifs that show up throughout *Smile*.

This is also, astonishingly, the first waltz the band ever recorded (sections of *Cabinessence*, which had not yet been released, are also in waltz time, as was part of an unreleased version of *Heroes & Villains*, but this is the first time an entire song is in 3/4). And Brian, Carl and Mike all add great vocals.

But lyrically, the song has a central problem. The lyrics are all pleas, of the form "let X, let Y, but don't let her go". This is a familiar form - e.g. *Blue Suede Shoes* ("you can knock me down, tread on my face, slander my name all over the place... but don't you step on my blue suede shoes").

But here, X and Y are all positive things - "let the bees make honey, let the poor find money, take away their sorrow, give them sunshine tomorrow, but don't take her out of my life..."

This avails itself of only two possible interpretations - either Mike Love is such a misanthrope that he hates bees, helping the poor, sunshine and so on, and is only willing to tolerate them if the nameless woman remains with him, or he is the greediest person in the world and wants the moon on a stick.

Great track anyway though.

How She Boogalooed It

Easily the worst song on the album, this track still has an important historical status, as it's the first original Beach Boys song (not counting surf instrumentals) that doesn't have a Brian Wilson co-writing credit. Credited to Love, Johnston, Jardine and Carl Wilson, with Jardine on lead vocals, this sounds like it was the result of a jam session with a couple of quick overdubs thrown on, and probably took slightly less time to write than it takes to listen to. All four co-writers would do better later.

Mama Says

Credited to Wilson and Love, this little vocal chant (the words "eat a lot, sleep a lot, brush 'em like crazy/run a lot, do a lot, never be lazy" repeated over and over) is a snippet that was originally part of *Vegetables*, and was recorded as such for *Smile*.

CD Bonus Tracks

Heroes & Villains (Alternate Take)

Not quite an alternate take, despite the title, the first part of this is identical to the single version as a performance, though a slightly different mix. But where the single goes into the chorus, this skips both the chorus and the 'la la la' verse, and goes straight into the *a capella* wordless verse (in what sounds like the same performance, but with either a very different mix or a different recording of at least Love's part).

We then move into a totally different piece of music - the 'cantina' section. This is a waltz time section (with an interpolated bar of common time), which returns to the dancing girl and the shooting from the first verse, over Western saloon-bar piano, with Brian and Mike trading off vocal lines, before ending with a jokey "You're under arrest!"

We then go back to familiar territory, going into the "my children were raised" section as used in the single, but where the single version ends "healthy, wealthy and wise" before tailing off in 'boys and girls and' vocals, this has a sharp edit and becomes "healthy, wealthy and often wise", with the piano coming in again on 'often'.

We then have half a verse over the same backing track

used for the first two verses - "at three score and five, I'm very much alive, I've still got the jive to survive with the heroes and villains" - before heavily echoed bass vocals and whistling are used to emulate the sound of a train picking up speed and going into the distance.

And to finish we have a vaguely cowboy-film sounding fade into the distance - pizzicato strings, acoustic guitar, harmonica, clip-clop percussion and wordless vocals in a variant of the verse musical material. In the entire song we haven't heard what became the chorus of the finished version. This version is, if anything, slightly superior to the finished one, but it's far less catchy and commercial.

Good Vibrations (Various Sessions)

This is a sequence of snippets from various sessions during the process of recording *Good Vibrations*, starting with the very first session and ending with a pieced together mostly-instrumental version of the track including a lot of unused sections, including an interesting fuzz-bass part and a gorgeous 'hum de ah' vocal harmony part.

Good Vibrations (Early Take)

This is the February 17th backing track with the February 18th guide vocal with Tony Asher's lyrics, as discussed in more detail in the main *Good Vibrations* section.

You're Welcome

The B-side of *Heroes & Villains*, this is a simple three-chord vocal chant with a ton of reverb, backed only with a glockenspiel and a bass drum, but is absolutely lovely.

Their Hearts Were Full Of Spring

Before the *Wild Honey* album was decided on, the Beach Boys (with Brian and minus Bruce) were going to release a live album called *Lei'd In Hawaii*, featuring *Smiley Smile*-esque arrangements. Unfortunately, the tapes were deemed unusable, even after a session of 'as live' re-recording. This recording is taken from the rehearsals for the live shows, and is an *a capella* recording of an old Four Freshmen song by Bobby Troup, which the group had already recorded with different lyrics as *A Young Man Is Gone*.

The song itself is a sentimental piece of nothing - it tries to encompass the lives of two people, but we're given no actual information about them except that they married, eventually died, and 'their hearts were full of spring', so have no real reason to care. The band do an exceptional job of the vocals, but it's not really worth a listen.

This song has been a staple of the band throughout its existence, from their first recordings through to today's touring version of the band, and so many more recordings of it exist, with two more official releases still to go (on *Live In London* and the *Good Vibrations: Thirty Years Of The Beach Boys* box set), and comparing versions by different line-ups can be interesting in showing the strengths and weaknesses of various vocalists, but other than that this is immensely skippable.

Can't Wait Too Long

In his liner notes for the *Smiley Smile/Wild Honey* twofer, David Leaf refers to this as the best piece of unreleased music in the Beach Boys' vaults, which suggests that he'd not listened to very much of it. Which isn't to say that this *Wild Honey*-era piece isn't nice, but most of it's just slight variations on a two-chord melodic idea originally sketched out during the *Smile* sessions. It's nicely arranged, with good vocals in the few sections where there are vocals (though an alternate version of this showed up on the *Good Vibrations: Thirty Years Of The Beach Boys* box set with more vocals), but it's nothing extraordinary. It does, however, at the end, feature a bass fade playing something very like the riff from *Shortenin' Bread* - a riff which we'll return to a lot in volumes two and three...

Friends/20/20

By 1968 the band were in the doldrums, commercially if not creatively. Experimenting with various gurus (some more dangerous than others) and allowing each member to write more of the material, the band were in such a state that on one tour they were playing to fewer than two hundred people per venue. At the same time, they were being treated as conquering heroes in Europe, where they were wildly popular - their tour of Czechoslovakia was so important in that country's culture that Tom Stoppard used it as a key point in his 2006 play about the Czech counterculture from the 1960s through to the Velvet Revolution, *Rock & Roll*.

The two albums on this release see them trying, in very different ways, to find a new place for themselves in a music world they'd helped revolutionise but which was already looking on them as past it.

Friends

One of the two albums Brian Wilson regularly cites as his favourite Beach Boys album (the other being *The Beach Boys Love You*) , this, rather than Wild Honey, is the logical next step after Smiley Smile. A set of more coherent, more tightly-produced songs, that still has the same gentleness, fragility and whimsy of that album. With more than half the songs lasting under two minutes, and many of them influenced by Transcendental Meditation, which a few of the band, especially Love, had taken up, this is one of the most highly-regarded of all the Beach Boys' albums (although Bruce Johnston loathes it).

This is also the first Beach Boys album to be released only in stereo[7] - another sign of Brian's waning influence in the group.

line-up

Brian Wilson, Carl Wilson, Dennis Wilson, Mike Love, Al Jardine, Bruce Johnston

Meant For You

At only thirty-nine seconds long, this is the shortest song in the Beach Boys' catalogue, but one of the loveliest - a Wilson/Love song with only organ and piano backing, as Mike sings "As I sit and close my eyes, there's peace in my mind, and I'm hoping that you'll find it too/and these feelings in my heart I know are meant for you".

Probably the first Love lyric inspired by Transcendental Meditation, this has little of the hectoring obviousness of some of his later TM songs, and is all the better for it. A genuinely welcoming, genuinely peaceful opener.

Friends

A lovely little waltz - one of many on this album - based around bass harmonica, vibraphone and acoustic guitar,

---

[7] A 'fold-down' mono mix of this was made, as was one for the next album, but these weren't separate mono mixes, just both stereo channels played through one channel.

FRIENDS

with a fuller sound than almost anything on the previous album, the credits for this - it's written by Brian, Carl, Mike and Al - show the first sign of a trend that would become apparent by the next album. More and more often Brian was coming up with fragmentary ideas - sometimes even finished songs, but often just partial songs - and leaving the rest of the band to flesh these out into full songs, as he became less and less inclined to be involved in the band.

Lyrically, this is a step back to the adolescent view - and language - of *All Summer Long* - "you told me when my girl was untrue/I loaned you money when the funds weren't too cool/I talked your folks out of making you cut off your hair" - but the sentiments, about the lasting power of friendship, were probably welcome for a band that had been on the brink of splitting recently.

Carl takes lead, and the most interesting thing musically is the semitone key-change between the first and second line of the verses. The whole thing is calming, but with just enough of interest in the arrangement to keep it from tipping over into the soporific.

Wake The World

A co-write by Brian and Al, this is Brian's first lead vocal on the album (with Mike and Carl assisting on the choruses), and is an unutterably beautiful one minute and twenty eight seconds. Just listen to the way the minor chords and strings in the descending bridge after "the light of the day is no longer here" turn into the relative major and the joyous horn part (my wife and I have been debating as to whether it's a euphonium or a tuba - definitely a saxhorn-type brass instrument, anyway) of the chorus. It's also one of several songs on this album to have as a strong component the I-IV-V standard progression - the songs on this album, more than on any other, are a strange mix of the sophisticated and the simplistic, in ways that can't obviously be put down to factors like the various collaborators on the songs.

This song was released as the B-side to the *Do It Again* single, and remained in the band's set in an even-more-abbreviated version for a year or two. A minor classic.

Be Here In The Mornin'

Another multi-author (Wilson/Wilson/Wilson/Love/Jardine) waltz, this consists of four distinct sections.

We start with a short, Hawaiian-sounding two-chord strum, with Brian singing wordlessly over it, before entering the verse. Contrary to David Leaf's CD liner notes, the verse isn't Brian singing - rather it's Al, singing a higher falsetto than Brian ever managed, over a very prominent bass, strummed acoustic guitar and very simple drums. The verse is easily the most harmonically interesting section, feinting at *Friends*' semitone key change after the first line, but going somewhere slightly different.

The chorus, with Carl singing lead and Al answering, both hugely phased, is much simpler harmonically, with no real surprises other than the Dsus4 chord ("make my life *whole*"). The almost-inaudible organ from the verse is much louder here, and a countermelody on tubular bells is introduced.

We then have a second verse (the Korthoff, Parks and Grillo mentioned are members of the band's management team - and see the credits for the next song) and chorus, before an eight-bar break consisting of single organ notes.

We then go back into the intro, but with Dennis rather than Brian singing the wordless vocal. We then have a final chorus, and an outro which is the same musical material as the intro, with Dennis again taking lead and the band harmonising, ending on a snare drum roll.

One of the less impressive songs on the album, this is still pleasant enough, and continues the mood set by the previous songs.

When A Man Needs A Woman

Written from the point-of-view of someone waiting for a son to be born (Brian and Marilyn were expecting what turned out to be their first daughter, Carnie), this is a charmingly simple (if mildly sexist - Brian doesn't seem to have considered that his first child could be anything other than a boy) country-flavoured song whose only deviation from the standard two-guitars-bass-drums line-up is a heavily reverbed 'ice-rink' Hammond organ that comes in on the instrumental break.

Harmonically simplistic in the verse, the chorus has a nice little chromatic run from G# up to D, and most of the variation in the song comes from repeating the same material in different keys (the song starts in C# for the verses, moves to D for the choruses, goes to C in the "a man needs a woman like a woman needs a man" section before going into a verse which leads to a final chorus in F# and a fade in C#).

A song this lyrically and musically simple, about something in Brian's personal life, with Brian the only Beach Boy heard vocally, might be expected to be a solo composition. Instead there are five credited writers here - Brian, Dennis, Al, Steve Korthoff and Jon Parks, the latter two part of the band's management.

Passing By

A short organ-led semi-instrumental, with Brian's wordless vocal singing a melody very similar in feel to many of the

Jack Nitzsche inspired instrumentals he'd earlier done, but with an arrangement very like the instrumental break of *When A Man Needs A Woman*.

This song originally had lyrics - "While walking down the avenue / I stopped to have a look at you / And then I saw / You're just passing by" - which more-or-less fit the verse vocal.

Anna Lee, The Healer

Mostly written by Love, though credited to Wilson/Love, this was written about a masseuse Love met while on a retreat with Maharishi Mahesh Yogi in Rishikesh (the same retreat where the Beatles wrote much of the White Album.) Much of Love's contribution to this album - and future albums - is inspired by his embracing of the Maharishi's teachings of Transcendental Meditation.

The verses are very simple, being based around the standard "Louie, Louie" I-IV-V-IV progression, with just Love singing over a piano and a bass (not, as David Leaf says in his liner notes, 'a piano bass line' - there are clearly two instruments on all but the first verse) with the band providing rudimentary harmonies. The chorus meanwhile starts with iii-IV-V-vi twice over, with the band singing block harmonies (with Brian singing a clearly strained falsetto on top, if it's not Al again). The only unusual points in the chord sequence are the I9 in the bridge and the iv on the lines going into and out of the chorus.

Little Bird

If you don't count *Denny's Drums*, this is Dennis Wilson's first songwriting credit without any of the rest of the band.

Written with lyricist Steve Kalinich, this is by far the best song on the album to this point.

Clearly very influenced by Brian's Smile music, this is harmonically simple, and based around a small number of sections, all of which are in turn based on two-chord repetitive phrases. The biggest influence is *Child Is Father Of The Man*, a then-unreleased *Smile* song whose arrangement and chord sequence is taken wholesale for the end of the song.

But this is still clearly a Dennis Wilson song. The meditative mood, the way it's built up out of independent sections that never quite repeat - this points the way to much of Dennis' later work. The arrangement (all muted trumpet, cello and banjo) might be his big brother's, but with this song Dennis was showing that he was soon going to be his brother's equal.

Dennis takes the lead, apart from the 'what a day' line, which Carl sings.

Be Still

The second Dennis Wilson/Kalinich song on the album, this is possibly the simplest thing the Beach Boys ever recorded. Each verse is just a I-IV phrase, repeated, then the whole thing repeated a tone up. The only instrument is an organ, holding chords down. And the only voice is Dennis, singing right at the top of his range, croaking rather than singing the higher notes.

A beautiful, delicate ballad, this would work well as a children's lullaby, sweet and innocent with no hint of darkness.

A word, though, on Steve Kalinich's lyrics. Kalinich will appear several times in volumes two and three of this series of books, and is far from my favourite lyricist - I may be very critical of him there. However, he's a friend of many of my friends, and they all say that once you know him as a person his lyrics seem much better. This is one of the few cases where I can see that. These lyrics (inspired by a line from Psalm 46 - "Be still and know that I am God") are simple and to the point, as many of Kalinich's lyrics are, without falling into cliché.

Between this and the previous song, *Friends* shows that even without Brian Wilson, Dennis' songwriting talent would be enough to make most bands jealous.

Busy Doin' Nothin'

With its bars of 5/4 half-way through otherwise 4/4 verses, and the odd bars of 7 we hear in the instrumental fade, this bossa nova piece is the most metrically irregular thing Brian Wilson has ever released.

One of only two Brian solo compositions on the album (the other being *Passing By*, this is musically the most complex piece on the album, full of VII9 and VI♭7(♭5) chords. Lyrically, however, it's another matter.

This is another of Brian's 'slice of life' songs, written about whatever he's thinking at the time, so we have lines like "I get a lot of thoughts in the morning, I write them all down/If it wasn't for that, I'd forget 'em in a while" in the verses, and the first chorus gives directions to drive to his house:

> Take all the time you need, it's a lovely night
>
> If you decide to come, you're gonna do it right
>
> Drive for a couple miles, you'll see a sign and turn left for a couple blocks, next is mine,
>
> You'll turn left on a little road, it's a bumpy one
>
> You'll see a white fence, move the gate and drive through on the left side

FRIENDS 157

> Come right in and you'll find me in my house somewhere
>
> Keeping busy while I wait

Brian's songs over the next few years would increasingly be of this nature. While unusual, this is still a stand-out track on the album, and one that could only have been written by Brian Wilson. Brian is the only vocalist on this track.

Diamond Head

A Hawaiian-flavoured instrumental, played on steel guitar, hand percussion and ukulele, this was apparently worked up in the studio, as the credit is split between Brian and session musicians Al Vescovo, Lyle Ritz and Jim Ackley.

A very simple collection of 'exotica'-sounding phrases, this sounds like a much bigger production than it in fact is, thanks to judicious use of reverb and sound effects.

The Hawaiian theme of this piece - plus the fact that it was briefly considered for a place in the 2004 *Smile* concerts, have led some to suggest that it was part of that album. But the recording dates, and the credits for the musicians, suggest otherwise.

Transcendental Meditation

A loud, rather dissonant, uptempo horn-driven song over a moronic riff, credited to Love, Jardine and Brian Wilson but mostly by the former, many fans of *Friends* think this song out of place. I disagree. While it's definitely a bit of a shock coming after so many gentle tracks, it still sounds of a piece with them, thanks to its short length, its repetitive, mantra-like nature, and its lyrical content. Far from the band's best album closer, it still fits nicely enough here, closing one of the band's best albums.

20/20

The Beach Boys' last studio album of the 1960s, and their last studio album of new material for Capitol, was a mixed bag of singles, cover versions and outtakes. So titled because it was their twentieth album (counting three 'best of' compilations) it's the last album they made under the intense deadline pressure they'd been under for the previous seven years - from now on, one album a year, at most, would be the norm.

It's notable as the major turning point for the band though. There are only five Brian Wilson songs on here, and four of those were either leftovers from earlier projects or intended for other people. Brian doesn't even appear on the cover. The band were going to have to learn how to cope without their leader...

line-up

Brian Wilson, Carl Wilson, Dennis Wilson, Mike Love, Al Jardine, Bruce Johnston

Do It Again

For the *Lei'd In Hawaii* project in 1967, Brian had come up with a new arrangement of the band's first single, *Surfin'*, featuring an organ riff based loosely on *Underwater* by The Frogmen, a surf instrumental that had been released on Candix records (the same label on which *Surfin'* had originally been released) in 1961.

Taking this riff and turning it into a vocal melody, Brian and Mike kept the surfing theme for this, their first surf record in four years (since *Don't Back Down* on the *All Summer Long* album). Produced by Brian and Carl, this has a curiously deadened sound, probably the result of one bounce-down too many, but the drum sound at the beginning is like nothing the band had ever recorded before.

One of the band's simplest hits (all on three chords apart from the middle eight, which adds in a few minor sevenths) the combination of the nostalgic lyrics ("let's get back together and do it again"), the opening drum part and the gorgeous middle eight melody brought this to number one in the UK - the band's second and final number one over here. In the US, it made number twenty - the band's last top twenty hit in the US for eight years.

The album version includes, on the fade, some 'woodshop' sound effects - these are from a recording done as part of the *Smile* sessions.

Mike sings lead, with Brian singing the wordless high falsetto.

I Can Hear Music

Carl Wilson's first solo production for the Beach Boys, this track was for a long time believed not to even feature Brian at all, though in fact he is in the harmony stack. Carl does an admirable job of replicating his production style, though on this cover of an obscure Ronettes track (the last song the Ronettes had released on Philles records, Phil Spector's record label).

Instrumentally, the track is simple, being mostly a bed of acoustic guitars and sleighbells, plus bass and drums (an electric piano was recorded, but I've seen people have huge arguments as to whether it's audible on the finished track at all. I come down on the 'audible' side, but it's so faint that even I have my doubts).

Vocally, however, it's extraordinary. The verses and choruses are just carried by Carl Wilson's lead vocal (one of the strongest he'd done thus far) with 'ooh' and 'aah' block backing vocals, but then there's an *a capella* section that's far and away the best Brian Wilson imitation arrangement the band ever did. While Carl keeps singing a standard lead vocal, the rest of the band chant the word 'music' over and over, while Mike sings "doh re mi fah so la ti do/I hear the music all the time now baby" in the bass register. The last great bit of harmony vocals the Beach Boys did in the 1960s.

Released as a single, this went to number 24 in the USA, and number 10 in the UK.

Bluebirds Over The Mountain

Written by Ersel Hickey (no relation to the current author), this is a nondescript 50s country song with frankly appalling lyrics ("A boy and girl they once fell in love/To each it seemed like heaven above/He looked into her eyes and said/Ooh-ee baby you're so good for my head") that Bruce Johnston liked for some reason. (The Beach Boys' version is actually slightly different lyrically to Hickey's original, but both are equally poor).

Johnston had recorded a rough backing track as a potential solo single, but when the band were desperate for material it was dusted off by Carl Wilson and turned into a group performance.

The result is a clash of four completely incompatible types of music. The song itself is a bad 50s number, but then the basic track is done in generic-Beach-Boys, with tuned percussion doubling the bass-line. But then, in an ill-advised nod to modernity, the band try to imitate Jimi

Hendrix and the other heavier rockers who were popular at the time, by getting touring band member Ed Carter to perform a squealing guitar solo all over it. And *then* we get a tag in which Johnston's lounge music tendencies come to the fore (Johnston would, a few years later, perpetrate *I Write The Songs*). Any two of these styles might - might - have worked together. Four of them on one single sounds like a game of Consequences gone seriously wrong.

Mike sings lead on the verses, Carl on the choruses and Bruce on the tag. Carl and Bruce produced, and the strings were arranged by Van McCoy (of *The Hustle* fame), who also arranged the strings on *Be With Me* and *The Nearest Faraway Place* on this album.

Be With Me

After the unimpressive previous track comes this, its polar opposite. Written and produced by Dennis, with as far as I can tell no participation by any of the other band members, here Dennis sings several vocal parts himself, over a moody, intense production unlike anything the band had done before, though still clearly indebted to his elder brother's work.

Harmonically very simple, mostly moving around i, iv and III in Gm with a brief key change to B♭ in the middle eight, everything here is geared around the production, all low throbbing bass and booming drums. This is the sound of desperation and frustration made audible.

The only minor flaw - if it is a flaw, and not intentional - is the double tracking error on the last verse, where Dennis simultaneously sings "set you free" and "set us free". Otherwise, this track shows again that Dennis was fast becoming the Wilson brother to watch out for, as a songwriter and producer.

All I Want To Do

Not to be confused with the similarly-named *All I Wanna Do* from the band's next album, *Sunflower*, this is an altogether more raucous affair, quite the loudest, rowdiest thing the band ever did, a four-chord rocker (apart from the orgasmic climax of ascending major chords before the last chorus and fade) by Dennis, driven by piano, saxophone and guitar. This is a much, much more convincing attempt at assimilating heavy rock than *Bluebirds*, and Mike Love turns in a performance unlike anything he'd done before or since, gruff and at times screaming.

I will never, ever forgive lyricist Steve Kalinich though, because Mike Love repeatedly sings the line "I just want to do it to you", and that's not an image I ever wanted in my head.

The very faint sounds at the end are apparently a recording of Dennis actually having sex with two groupies in the recording studio. According to engineer Steve Desper, this didn't record properly the first time and Dennis insisted on a second take...

The Nearest Faraway Place

An instrumental for electric piano and string section by Bruce Johnston, this is the kind of thing that gives elevator music a bad name. Saccharine, over-orchestrated, and pointless, this is tuneful enough in its way, but has no real reason for existing.

Cotton Fields (The Cotton Song)

An old Leadbelly song suggested by Al Jardine, who wrote the additional verses about 'a nice old man, he had a hat on' and sings lead, this is a Brian Wilson production but shares the curiously flat sound of much of this album, although there's some nice banjo work. The band would re-record this the next year, with Al producing and a more dynamic arrangement, and it would be a hit in most countries outside the US (that version is on the *Good Vibrations: Thirty Years Of The Beach Boys* box set, which I deal with in volume two).

I Went To Sleep

This Brian and Carl Wilson composition was recorded for *Friends* but unaccountably left off. Another slice-of-life song, this time about walking to the park on a sunny day and falling asleep in the grass, this is a lovely little waltz, with a flute-let instrumental track and lush ninth chords, and with beautiful harmonies by the band (and listen out for the snoring sounds during the instrumental break). It also shares a few melodic ideas with the next song.

Time To Get Alone

Another Brian Wilson song, another leftover from a previous project. This was originally recorded in 1967 by Redwood, the band that became Three Dog Night, but according to Chuck Negron of that band, Brian was bullied by the rest of the Beach Boys into giving the song to them.

Recorded over the same backing track as that version (Steve Desper apparently disputes this, but my ears say otherwise), Carl Wilson produced the vocals, in an expansion of Brian's original three-vocalist arrangement.

Despite whatever acrimony may have been involved, the result is lovely. One of Brian's simplest songs, this is very much in the mould of other 'escape' songs like *In My Room*, and one's heart breaks on hearing the lines "just away, away from the people, and safe from the people". But unlike many of Brian's other 'scared' songs, this time he's going away *with* someone, and that comfort and security comes through in every note of this gorgeous harpsichord-based waltz.

Because of its origins, this is the 'arty' mid-60s Brian Wilson sound, with harpsichord, strings and vibraphone, but with the lusher vocals of the late-60s albums. Carl and Brian sing lead. A minor masterpiece.

Never Learn Not To Love

And here we get to a song it's almost impossible now to review dispassionately, and to hear as it must have sounded when it first came out.

While this is credited to Dennis Wilson, it was actually largely written by a friend of Dennis', who asked that his name not be put on the record's credits. That friend, Charles Manson, was leader of a hippie commune who within a few months of this record's release were responsible for a series of horrific murders that became one of the most well-known crimes of the twentieth century. (Dennis had cut off all ties with Manson some time earlier, and was as horrified as anyone, and more so than most, at his crimes).

While it's not the business of this book to judge the band's private lives, in this case the behind-the-scenes story is so awful it's simply impossible to objectively assess the song. I would be doing my readers a disservice to treat this as just another Beach Boys song and look at the chord changes without taking into account that it's by a murderer, even if I could, but my perception of this song is tied up with my perception of Manson. Would I find lines like "submission is a gift, give it to your lover" as creepy had they actually been written by Wilson? I don't know.

It's long been rumoured that Manson helped with some of Dennis' other songs from this period too, but this is the only one for which there's definite proof.

For that reason, I'll have to recuse myself from discussing this track - I want neither to damn a performance and production that had a lot of work put into it, nor to be seen to be praising something whose major creator was a mass murderer.

Our Prayer

And as if to provide a spiritual cleansing after the unpleasantness of Manson, comes this beautiful piece.

A pastiche of Bach's choral work, this wordless *a capella* hymn was written by Brian Wilson as the introduction to *Smile*, and is every bit as beautiful as one would imagine a Brian Wilson pastiche of Bach to be.

Recorded in 1966, the band thickened the sound with additional overdubs and reverb in 1968, but either version is among the most beautiful vocal music ever recorded.

Cabinessence

And the last song on the album is by far the best, a track originally intended for *Smile*. Written by Brian and Van Dyke Parks, this had been completely recorded for Smile, except for the lead vocal, which was added by Carl in 1968.

The result is astonishing, one of the best things the band ever did - which is to say it is one of the best musical recordings of the twentieth century. Parks' punning, Joycean lyrics contrast an idyllic 'home on the range' in the verses with the 'iron horse', the railway that made the West possible, in the choruses, before at the end focusing on the immigrant labour that had built that railway. In the context of *Smile* these lyrics are much more powerful, referring back to other songs which in turn refer to this one, but even taken as a song on its own, divorced from its intended context, and placed near the end of a patchy collection like this, it still retains its power.

The verse, in 4/4 time, starts with just a banjo, evoking the old west, and Brian singing an ascending scalar phrase, singing 'doing doing' over and over in imitation of the banjo, while Carl sings in his gentlest, purest tones, as bass and piano come in, before everything drops out except a harmonica and a harmonium, playing variations of the trumpet part from *Heroes & Villains*, but in counter-movement to each other, for two bars.

This musical material then repeats, before entering into a two chord waltz-time chorus with an utterly different feel. Over clanking percussion, representing the spikes being driven into the ground to hold the rails together, the band chant 'who ran the iron horse?' over and over, while a wailing falsetto Brian, fuzz bass and cellos race each other up and down ascending and descending scales, in much the same manner as in the similar-sounding *Smile* track *Mrs O'Leary's Cow*, but much more frenzied, before collapsing back, exhausted, into the comfort of the verse.

After the second verse, we get another chorus, but this time with an additional element. Dennis is now singing a totally different, unconnected set of lyrics. These are buried in the mix, but I've reproduced them below:

> Truck driving man do what you can
>
> High-tail your load off the road
>
> Out of night-life-it's a gas man
>
> I don't believe I gotta grieve
>
> In and out of luck

> With a buck and a booth
>
> Catching on to the truth
>
> In the vast past, the last gasp
>
> In the land in the dust
>
> Trust that you must
>
> Catch as catch can

We then enter a little, gentle, round as the band sing "Have you seen the grand coolie working on the railroad?" (the use of 'coolie' here an unfortunate oversight on the part of Parks, who is usually far more sensitive to the connotations of his words, but presumably was too enamoured of the pun on the Grand Coulee Dam and its resonances with the other themes of *Smile*) over a tinkling waltz, before the cellos come back in, in one of the most beautiful, and complex, pieces of contrapuntal vocals the band ever recorded.

And then over cello, banjo and harmonica, while the tinkling percussion continues, Love starts singing "Over and over the crow cries uncover the cornfield". This line apparently caused one of the biggest arguments in the recording of *Smile*, when the literal-minded Love kept questioning Parks as to the literal meaning of the line, and Parks was unable or unwilling to provide him with one. Nonetheless, Love eventually did sing it, and sing it beautifully. Then the band start singing those up-and-down fast scales again, as a fuzz bass comes in, and the banjo gets steadily more distorted til at the end the banjo sounds exactly like a sitar.

As the Beach Boys' last Capitol studio album ends, there's almost a sense of "*This* is what you're giving up", as a song from two years in the past points the way to the next two albums in the future.

CD Bonus Tracks

Break Away

The Beach Boys' last single for Capitol for nearly twenty years was this, other than *Good Vibrations* possibly their finest 60s single.

Co-written by Brian and his father Murry Wilson (under the pseudonym Reggie Dunbar), on first listening this is a cheerful, upbeat song about escaping from all one's worries - many have interpreted it as being at least in part about the band being released from their onerous contract with Capitol. It's only on closer examination that it becomes clear that it is, at least in part, about trying to escape from mental illness:

> When I lay down on my bed
>
> I hear voices in my head
>
> Telling me now, hey, it's only a dream
>
> The more I thought of it
>
> I have been out of it
>
> And here's the answer I found instead
>
> It's in my head...

Coming from someone who would spend much of the next few decades being tortured by those 'voices in [his] head', this is no longer quite so cheerful - and the historical knowledge that Brian wouldn't 'break away' from his problems makes this all the more heartbreaking; doubly so when you consider that the song was co-written by the father who was the cause of so many of those problems.

Nonetheless, the song itself is upbeat, cheerful and exhilarating. Never a favourite of the band (Johnston believes the vocals, which are slowed down from the original recording, make them sound like old men, while Jardine considers it underproduced) their views may be tainted by the fact that the single did nothing at all on the US chart - though in the UK it made number 6 and was one of their biggest hits.

Carl sings lead on the verses, Brian on the first bridge, and Al on the choruses (another example of these three sounding spookily similar), while Mike sings the prominent bass vocal on the tag and the second bridge. A simplistic song, this is all in the vocal arrangement and performance, which are some of the best the band would ever do.

Celebrate The News

The B-side to *Breakaway*, by Dennis and his friend and frequent collaborator Gregg Jakobson, is on such a similar theme it's almost like the two brothers had deliberately decided to write complementary songs. While harmonically simple - it's based around repeating two-chord shuffles between chords a fifth apart, with the patterns themselves moving up and down in whole-tone steps much like his brother's 1965 and 1966 work - this manages to throw off expectations by keeping a constant pulse but varying the stresses in such a way that without changing tempo at all he manages to switch between 6/4 and 4/4 time signatures, confusing one's time sense.

A very 'Dennis' song, with its throbbing bass and pounding kettle drums, this is a far more visceral record than Brian's more cerebral A-side, but it's hard to say that one approach is better than another. As Brian was becoming less and less involved with the band, Dennis was rapidly taking his place as a songwriter and producer worth paying attention to.

We're Together Again

A *Friends* era outtake, co-credited to Brian and Ron Wilson (no known relation to Brian, this is not the more famous Surfaris drummer of the same name, but someone for whom Brian produced an unsuccessful single around this time. One presumes he is also not the even more famous Ronald Wilson Reagan, of whom more, sadly, in volume two). Some versions credit just R. Wilson, and it is actually hard to see how this song could have taken two people to write, but it does have enough of Brian's fingerprints on it that I find it hard to imagine that he had no part in its writing.

A very simple song that sounds unfinished, this is another song built around I-IV chords in the chorus, with a slight variation of the doo-wop sequence for the verse, and a middle eight built around IV and ii. The most 'Brian' section comes towards the end, when the two-chord chorus phrase is repeated, each time a semitone up, before dropping back to its original key for the fade.

Carl and Brian appear to be the only Beach Boys on this track, but one suspects it inspired Bruce Johnston to write the very similar *Deirdre*, which would appear on the *Sunflower* album.

Walk On By

A fragment, barely forty seconds long, of the Bacharach/David song, with Brian singing the lead up to 'foolish pride', where Dennis takes over and immediately forgets the words, and busks through with just 'aah's, til the band come in with a full vocal part for "I break down and cry", at which point the track ends. It's interesting to hear this sophisticated piece done in the laid-back, stripped-down style the Beach Boys were using at the time, but this isn't even an attempt at a proper recording.

Old Folks At Home/Ol'Man River

This, on the other hand, is a fully-fledged-out arrangement that wouldn't have been out of place on *Smile*. Starting with a simple statement of the "Swanee River" melody on the piano (another appearance for a song - and a song-writer - that had influenced much of Brian's work already) the song goes into an uptempo version of *Ol' Man River*, with a *Smile*-esque run up and down a chromatic scale on a cello to bridge the two. The *Ol' Man River* arrangement goes between just acoustic guitar and bass, and a fuller band with drums and tack piano, and with a harmonica and trombone playing off each other.

And the harmonica and trombone are echoed in the vocals, by Brian and Mike respectively - oddly the only two band members who appear vocally. These were clearly guide vocals however - there are multiple Brians sketching out hesitant vocal lines, and points where Mike forgets his words - but there's the essence of a great arrangement there. One of the best unreleased bonus tracks out of all the 'twofer' CDs. (It's worth noting that there are two slightly different mixes of this track available, depending on if you buy the 1990 release of this CD or the 2001 re-release. Anything you purchase from an MP3 store or listen to on an internet streaming site will be the latter.)

Beach Boys Concert/Live In London

And finally for this book, we come to a CD containing two very different live albums, one from 1964, when the band were at the height of their success at home and featuring the 'classic' line-up, and one from 1968, when the band would play to barely 200 people in the US, but were hugely popular in Europe.

The interesting thing, comparing these two albums, is that though they were recorded only four years apart, they don't share a single song in common. That's how fast the Beach Boys were moving creatively, and indeed how fast the music industry was moving.

I'll deal with these albums in a little less depth than the studio albums, because I've dealt with most of the songs in their studio versions.

Beach Boys Concert

The band's first live album is only partly actually live. Recorded at a show in Sacramento, the album was substantially re-worked in the studio, and at least a couple of the tracks are in fact remixed versions of the studio releases with audience noise overdubbed, rather than live recordings.

That said, this was not because the Beach Boys were incapable of sounding like this live. The DVD *The Lost Concert*, released in the late 1990s, is a true live recording of a substantially similar setlist from a few months earlier, and on there the band sound, if anything, better than on these retouched recordings. This isn't a truly live album, but nor is it a dishonest one - if you went to see the Beach Boys live in 1964 this is pretty much what you would have heard, screams and all. Certainly it pleased the band's fans enough that it went to number one in the album charts.

line-up

Brian Wilson, Carl Wilson, Dennis Wilson, Mike Love, Al Jardine

Fun, Fun, Fun

After an introduction by the band's promoter Fred Vail, pasted in from a different show (the original recording has him saying 'a gala *Christmas* concert' we get this, the studio recording of this track sped up, without the organ overdubs, and with a lot of screaming girls and a very obvious edit into a sudden 'thump' at the end.

The Little Old Lady From Pasadena

A hit for the band's friends and frequent collaborators Jan & Dean, this rather silly song about an old lady who likes drag racing was written by Jan Berry, Roger Christian and Berry's roommate Don Altfeld. Love takes lead, with Brian singing falsetto and Carl doing a very reasonable guitar solo.

This song remains in the setlist of the current touring 'Beach Boys' to this day.

Little Deuce Coupe

This live version has always been the source of much mockery from Beach Boys fans, because Mike introduces the instruments one at a time, "we start with Denny on the drums" (drums are heard) "then Al with the rhythm guitar" (drums are heard...), leading to rumours that Al's guitar wasn't plugged in.

In actual fact, Jardine's guitar is audible on the track, but only faintly. This routine can be seen and heard, much more clearly, on The Lost Concert DVD.

The actual performance is a perfectly competent performance of the song, raw enough that one can easily believe it's a genuinely live recording, and with Jardine's vocal high in the mix.

Long Tall Texan

A comedy country song by Henry Strzelecki, a musical relative of *Hi-Heeled Sneakers*, this is most notable for the weird yodelling noise Mike, who takes lead, makes at the end of every verse. This would be recorded by the band again for their final album, 1996's *Stars And Stripes Vol. 1*, where country singer Doug Supernaw took lead.

In My Room

A lovely performance, quite possibly redone in the studio.

Monster Mash

A cover of a then-recent hit by Bobby "Boris" Pickett and the Crypt-Kickers, this song was later made famous by the Bonzo Dog Band. A comedy dance number, Love does a quite wonderful "Igor" voice here.

Let's Go Trippin'

Pretty much the same as the studio version, but slightly faster.

Papa-Oom-Mow-Mow

A cover of the Rivingtons' song, the band would rerecord this the next year for *Beach Boys Party*. Both versions do the song rather more justice than it deserves, between Brian's yelping and squealing falsetto and Love's growled 'papa oom mow mow' bass.

The Wanderer

A cover of the Dion song, with Dennis on lead, when the band played this live Dennis would come up front and Brian would take over the drums. The perfect song for Dennis to sing, this not only fit his playboy image but had a fairly limited vocal range.

Hawaii

An improvement on the studio version, mostly because Mike doesn't have a cold, this is taken at a faster tempo and has a lot more energy.

Graduation Day

See the description under the *Today!/Summer Days...And Summer Nights* bonus tracks, but note that the harmonies are harsher here, and there are various noises of the band laughing, hitting wrong notes etc.

I Get Around

A stripped down mix of the single version, without the organ overdubs and guitar solo, but with the handclaps during instrumental sections that prove it couldn't possibly be live.

Johnny B Goode

And the album ends with a cover of the Chuck Berry classic whose guitar part the band had 'borrowed' for the opening song. Taken at a ridiculously fast pace, and with what sounds like Brian and Mike doubling each other on lead, this sounds like pretty much every garage band cover of this song you've ever heard.

Live In London

Unlike the previous album, this recording is genuinely live, being an edited version of two shows recorded in 1968 at the Finsbury Park Astoria, London (minus *All I Want To Do*, which was played as an encore but was cut). This shows the band augmented by outside musicians, but these musicians would be associated with the band for many years - Ed Carter would play with the Beach Boys both in the studio and live until the late 1990s and still plays with Al Jardine's live band, Mike Kowalski played with the band off and on until 2007, and Daryl Dragon would stay with the band until the early 1970s, when he would launch a successful career as 'the Captain' in The Captain And Tenneille.

The band's setlist had totally changed over the four years between live albums, and this one only contains two pre-*Pet Sounds* tracks, both from 1965. In a very real sense this is the work of a totally different, much more polished, band. Even so, much of it is fudged, with complicated bits glossed over - simply because it's not possible for a small number of people to reproduce those records accurately.

Another difference between this album and the earlier one, though, is the absence of Brian Wilson, who was no longer a touring member of the band. His vocals have been shared out between the rest of the band, and it's interesting how well Carl and Al can double for him in their respective ranges.

line-up

Carl Wilson, Dennis Wilson, Mike Love, Al Jardine, Bruce Johnston, with Ed Carter (bass/guitar), Mike Kowalski (drums) and Daryl Dragon (keyboards) plus unknown horn players

Darlin'

A very creditable first track, sounding pretty much like the record except for the drumming, which has far more hi-hat, and Mike's interjections (a little counter-vocal in the second verse, and a comedy growl)

Wouldn't It Be Nice

Obviously missing the layers of instrumentation and the multiply-overdubbed vocals, the band have to strain for a few high notes on the 'run, run, ri-oooh' sections. They also cut out a huge chunk of the song, going straight from the middle eight to the 'good night baby' section, without having to deal with the complicated tempo changes of the "you know it seems the more we talk about it" parts. They're bluffing their way through, and trading sophistication for excitement, but it works.

Al takes Brian's vocal part here, and does an admirable job, sounding enough like Brian that you could believe it was the same singer, but with a fullness to his vocals that Brian could rarely manage in this range.

Sloop John B

For this, the second *Pet Sounds* track in a row, Carl takes his brother's vocal part. The flute part is played by one of the session players, and the horn section do a competent job of filling out the rest of the instruments. The *a capella* section is skipped.

California Girls

The instrumental intro of this is severely curtailed. On the choruses, rather than the complicated overlapping harmonies, the band just sing in unison, but they do manage to reproduce the counterpoint on the tag. This is the earliest song the band play in this show.

Do It Again

At the time this was recorded, this was a recent UK number one hit. Brian's falsetto part here is replaced by a horn line, but otherwise there's nothing on the record that they don't manage to pull off here.

Wake The World

Performed in total darkness, with some locker room banter before the start, this has Carl singing Brian's part and Al singing Carl's part. For some reason it starts half-way through the first verse, but otherwise this is a stunningly close recreation of the original arrangement, and one of the more impressive performances on the album.

Aren't You Glad

An odd choice for a live show, this is one of the best tracks on the album, with Love giving a vocal easily the equal of his studio performance, and Jardine covering for both Brian Wilson and those parts where Carl Wilson sang two vocal lines on the record.

Bluebirds Over The Mountain

An improvement on the studio version, thanks to it sounding like a coherent arrangement, this is still the weakest song on the album. The best thing about it is Mike's fast-talking Spanish intro.

Their Hearts Were Full Of Spring

A nice performance of a terrible song, this song remains in the set list of the touring 'Beach Boys' to this day. As does Mike Love's '*a capella*, which means nude' joke. This is taken faster than the versions with Brian singing, and is the best of the officially released versions of this song.

Good Vibrations

You have to feel sorry for the band for even thinking about performing this one live, but they pull it off extraordinarily well. Taken at a slightly faster tempo than on the record, obviously they don't have the cello, jews harp and so on, but the cello parts are pulled off very well on guitar, Brian's falsetto is hardly missed, and apart from Mike's annoying joking on the 'gotta keep' section (which is extended, and the band sing 'with you' rather than 'with her'), there's barely a wrong note here. No, it's not as good as the record, but given the corners they've cut on other songs here, it's rather astonishing how close they come on easily the most difficult song to pull off.

God Only Knows

The first of two encore songs, on this the band (as they would for the remainder of their career), skip the staccato section, but it's made up for by a Carl Wilson vocal that's even better than on the record (listen to the first "so what good would living do me?"). Carl and Al sing Brian's parts and Mike doubles Bruce.

Barbara Ann

It's *Barbara Ann*, what do you expect? On the plus side, this has Al singing rather than Dean Torrence, and the band are mostly singing the same words as each other...

CD Bonus Tracks

Don't Worry Baby

An outtake from the show recorded for the *Concert* album, this is the only officially-released live version of this song with Brian in his 60s prime voice. Much better than some of the material that was used on the album, it was presumably cut because of Mike Love telling the audience "you're bitchin' as usual" during the intro.

Heroes & Villains

From the *Lei'd In Hawaii* shows, the only times Brian ever sang lead on this song with the Beach Boys, this is quite a special version, arranged in the style of the rest of *Smiley Smile*, stripped down to just organ, bass and drums, but keeping the structure of the single version. Some of the loveliest vocals on the entire CD are on this track.

References

Books

Much of this book is based on information picked up from discussions over sixteen years, as while there are many, many books on the Beach Boys, very few actually concentrate on the band's music, preferring instead to concentrate on the tabloid aspects of the band's life.

There are a few exceptions though. The following books are accessible enough to be of interest to the casual fan, while still accurate and interesting enough to keep the more dedicated fan happy.

The Complete Guide To The Music Of The Beach Boys by Andrew Doe and John Tobler (Omnibus Press) is a good, if too-short (due to formatting restrictions) overview of the band's career.

Inside the Music Of Brian Wilson, by Philip Lambert (Continuum) is an extremely in-depth look at, specifically, Brian Wilson's 1962-1969 musical output.

Back To The Beach: A Brian Wilson And The Beach Boys Reader , ed. Kingsley Abbot, (Helter Skelter) is a collection of essays by various people on the band's music and lives. The quality varies enormously, but is far better than one might expect.

Look, Listen, Vibrate, Smile! by Domenic Priore, (Last Gasp) is a collection of vintage newspaper articles and new essays by Priore and others. If you can, though, get one of the earlier editions of this book - Priore has a tendency to present his own hypotheses as fact, and this increases in later editions.

There are many biographies of the band and its members, and these are mostly outside the scope of this book, dealing as they do with the band's personal life. However, **Catch A Wave, The Rise, Fall And Redemption Of The Beach Boys' Brian Wilson**, by Peter A Carlin (Rodale) is the least sensationalised of these I have come across. And Jon Stebbins has authored two very good biographies of individual band members - **Dennis Wilson: The Real Beach Boy** (ECW) and, (with David Marks), **The Lost Beach Boy** (Virgin), both of which combine readability with accuracy in a way that is otherwise almost unknown among Beach Boys books.

DVDs

A few excellent DVDs exist covering this period. **The Lost Concert** is a 1964 live show with Brian, Al, Carl, Dennis and Mike.

The definitive video biography of the band is Alan Boyd's 1999 documentary **Endless Harmony**, which despite being an authorised biography with the full participation of all the surviving members of this most litigious of groups manages to tell the story accurately and entertainingly.

Don Was' 1995 film **I Just Wasn't Made For These Times** is a wonderfully moving documentary about Brian Wilson, with participation from Van Dyke Parks and Carl Wilson among others. This often comes on DVD paired with the 1980s documentary **An American Band**, which has more or less been superseded by Boyd's film, but is still worth watching.

And the DVDs **Brian Wilson Presents Pet Sounds Live In London** and **Brian Wilson Presents Smile** have, along with their extraordinarily good live performances of those albums, very decent documentaries by Wilson's friend and biographer David Leaf. Both documentaries do verge on the idolatrous, and relegate the rest of the band to footnotes, but they are still definitely worth watching.

Websites

Andrew Doe's Bellagio site,
   http://www.esquarterly.com/bellagio/ , is undoubtedly the best resource for checking matters of pure fact about the band.
   Francis Greene's chord transcriptions, available from http://www.surfermoon.com/tabs.shtml, made the difference between this book being possible and impossible.

Index

'Til I Die., 69
20/20, 149, 158
2JN, 115

409, 16, 21, 26, 42

A Christmas Gift To You, 61
A Hard Day's Night *(Beatles album)*, 91
A Mighty Wind, 96
A Postcard From California *(album)*, 12
A Thing Or Two, 141
A Young Man Is Gone, 44, 147
Abbot, Kingsley, 99, 183
About Time, 124
Ackley, Jim, 157
Ad Libs, the, 76, 123
After The Game, 73, 85
Airplane, 71
All Dressed Up For School, 54
All I Wanna Do, 162
All I Want To Do, 162, 177
All Summer Long (album), 39, 45, 65, 71, 151, 159
All Summer Long (song), 48
Alley Oop, 94
Alpert, Herb, 16
Altfeld, Don, 174
American Graffitti, 49
Amusement Parks USA, 76
An American Band, 184
And Your Dream Comes True, 86
Anna Lee, The Healer, 154
Araiza, Tilt, 104
Archies, The, 16
Aren't You Glad, 140, 180
Asher, Tony, 17, 100, 102–104, 112–114, 116, 120, 122, 146
At The Hop, 52
Atkins, Chet, 51
Auld Lang Syne, 61
Australia, 32

Baa Baa Black Sheep, 86
Bach, Johann Sebastian, 68, 165
Bacharach, Burt, 82, 108, 170
Back To The Beach: A Brian Wilson And The Beach Boys Reader, 183
Baker, Adrian, 119
Ballad Of Ole' Betsy, 40, 43
Banana (dog), 117
Barbara Ann, 96, 182
Barnyard, 131
Barry, Jeff, 77
Barry, John, 116
Basie, William "Count", 83
Bates, Leroy, 95
Baxter, Les, 115
Be Here In The Mornin', 152
Be My Baby, 33, 70, 71
Be Still, 155
Be True To Your School, 40, 54
Be With Me, 161
Beach Boys Concert, 57, 63, 92, 173, 182
Beach Boys Party, 78, 89, 176
Beach Boys, post-1998 touring band, 30, 54, 103, 114, 147, 175, 181
Beatles, the, 11, 15, 32, 35, 45, 49, 54, 71, 75, 78, 79, 81, 83, 91, 99, 137, 154
Berry, Chuck, 10, 14, 20, 21, 29, 32, 52, 177
Berry, Jan, 21, 174
Big Sur, 143
Blaine, Hal, 37, 47, 65, 77, 90, 115, 122, 125
Blake, Ginger, 54
Blossoms, the, 67
Blue Christmas, 60
Blue Moon, 35
Blue Suede Shoes, 144
Bluebirds Over The Mountain, 160, 162, 180
Bob. B. Soxx And The Blue Jeans, 50

INDEX

Bobby "Boris" Pickett and the Crypt-Kickers, 176
Bonzo Dog Band, the, 176
Boogie Woodie, 31
Bowie, David, 129
Boyd, Alan, 184
Brahms, Johannes, 49
Break Away, 168
Breakaway, 169
Breedlove, Craig, 43
Brian Wilson Presents Pet Sounds Live In London, 184
Brian Wilson Presents Smile, 184
Brian Wilson Reimagines Gershwin, 12
Brown, Buster, 69
Brown, Charles, 59
Bryant, Felice and Boudleaux, 93
Bull Session With The Big Daddy, 75
Busy Doin' Nothin', 156
Butler, Billy, 22
Byrds, The, 47

Cabinessence, 129, 143, 165
California Girls, 17, 52, 81, 86, 102, 111, 124, 131, 179
Call Any Vegetable, 133
Campbell, Glen, 64, 65, 112
Can I Get A Witness, 51, 123
Can't Wait Too Long, 147
Candix, 17
Candix records, 158
Cannon, Freddie 'Boom Boom', 15, 76
Capitol Records, 11, 14–16, 32, 127, 158, 167, 168
Capp, Frank, 65, 114
Captain Beefheart, 18
Car Crazy Cutie, 41, 58
Carl's Big Chance, 49, 51, 123
Carlin, Peter Ames, 184
Carlo, Andrea, 15
Carol (Chuck Berry song), 32
Caroline, No, 100, 116, 137
Carter, Ed, 161, 177, 178
"Cassius" Love vs "Sunny" Wilson, 34
Castells, the, 38
Catch A Wave, 27, 30
Catch A Wave, The Rise, Fall And Redemption Of The Beach Boys' Brian Wilson, 184
Celebrate The News, 169
Celebration, 136
Chaplin, Blondie, 11
Charles, Ray, 83

Cherry, Cherry Coupe, 24, 42
Child Is Father Of The Man, 155
Chordettes, the, 132
Christian, Roger, 21, 27, 29, 33, 34, 40–43, 45, 174
Christmas Day, 60, 69
Chug-A-Lug, 15
Cindy, Oh Cindy, 24
Clark, Dick, 52
Coasters, the, 90
Cochrane, Eddie, 18
Cole, Jerry, 102
Coleman, Gary, 108
Columbia Records, 76
Costello, Elvis, 107
Cottonfields, 87, 96, 162
Country Air, 141
County Fair, 15, 76
Cowsill, John, 103
Cowsills, the, 103
Crystals, the, 38, 67, 77, 95
Cuckoo Clock, 18
Custom Machine, 44

Da Doo Ron Ron, 141
Dale, Dick, 20, 23, 84
Dance, Dance, Dance, 55, 70, 87
Danny and the Juniors, 52
Dante And His Friends, 16
Dante, Ron, 16
Darlin', 89, 141, 178
David, Hal, 170
Day Tripper, 35
de Lory, Al, 102, 125
Dean, James, 44
Deirdre, 170
Dennis Wilson: The Real Beach Boy, 184
Denny's Drums, 37, 154
Denny, Martin, 115
Derbyshire, Delia, 124
Desert Drive, 78
Desper, Steve, 162, 163
Devoted To You, 93, 95
Diamond Head, 157
DiMucci, Dion, 16, 36, 41, 176
Dino, Desi and Billy, 92
Do It Again, 19, 152, 158, 180
Do You Remember?, 52
Do You Wanna Dance?, 66, 74
Doctor Who, 124
Doe, Andrew, 9, 183, 185
Doggett, Bill, 22
Domino, Antoine "Fats", 29, 85

INDEX

Don't Back Down, 54, 56, 159
Don't Go Near The Water, 96
Don't Hurt My Little Sister, 67
Don't Talk (Put Your Head On My Shoulder), 83, 106, 110, 116, 137
Don't Worry Baby, 33, 35, 48, 182
Dorman, Harold, 92
Douglas, Steve, 65
Dragon, Daryl, 178
Drive In, 52
Dunbar, Reggie (Murry Wilson), 168
Dylan, Bob, 95, 129

Eddy, Duane, 31
Endless Harmony (album), 11, 123
Endless Harmony (film), 184
Endless Summer, 45, 80
Everly Brothers, the, 93

Fall Breaks And Back To Winter (Woody Woodpecker Symphony), 133
Fannie Mae, 69, 78, 135
Farmer's Daughter, 20, 23
Fassert, Fred, 96
Finders Keepers, 23
Fire, 133
Fitzgerald, Ella, 83
Fleetwood Mac, 20
Flight of the Bumble-bee, 31
Foggy Notion, 50
Foster, Stephen, 28
Four Freshmen, the, 26, 28, 36, 40, 44, 57, 84, 86, 88, 96, 147
Four Seasons, the, 30, 84
Fowley, Kim, 94
Frazer, Dallas, 94
Freeman, Bobby, 66
Friends (album), 106, 149, 156, 157, 170
Friends (song), 150, 152
Frogmen, the, 158
Frosty The Snowman, 60
Fun, Fun, Fun, 22, 27, 32, 37, 174

Gamblers, the, 18
Ganz Allein, 37
Gaye, Marvin, 51
Get A Job, 134
Gettin' Hungry, 136, 141
Gettin' In Over My Head (album), 78
Girl Don't Tell Me, 78, 84
Girls On The Beach, 52
God Only Knows, 27, 69, 100, 104, 110, 120, 138, 181

Good To My Baby, 67
Good Vibrations, 104, 112, 119, 121, 122, 124, 126, 131, 132, 135, 146, 168, 181
Good Vibrations (Early Take), 146
Good Vibrations (Various Sessions), 120, 146
Good Vibrations: Thirty Years Of The Beach Boys (box set), 17, 83, 123, 127, 147, 148, 163
Goodman, Benny, 105
Gordon, Jim, 65, 110, 122
Graduation Day, 36, 84, 88, 177
Grainer, Ron, 124
Granata, Charles, 99
Greene, Francis, 185
Greenwich, Ellie, 77
Grillo, Nick, 152
Guitar Man, 139

Haley, Bill, 139
Hang on to your ego, 112
Harrison, George, 71, 112
Hawaii, 54, 176
Hawaii (song), 30, 41
Hawthorne, CA (album), 11, 29, 94
He Gives Speeches, 133
Heads You Win, Tails I Lose, 18, 23
Heart And Soul, 35
Help (Beatles album), 75
Help Me, Rhonda, 69, 78, 80, 135
Help Me, Ronda, 69
Hendrix, Jimi, 161
Here Comes The Night, 143
Here Today, 112, 120
Heroes And Villains, 55, 129, 131, 133, 137, 143, 145, 146, 166, 182
Heroes And Villains (Alternate Take), 145
Hey Little Cobra, 64
Hi-Heeled Sneakers, 175
Hickey, Ersel, 160
Hide Go Seek, 56
Hinsche, Annie, 92
Hinsche, Billy, 90, 92
Holidays, 117
Holland, 143
Hollywood Argyles, the, 94
Hondells, the, 38, 46
Honeys, the, 28, 54, 56, 91
Honky Tonk (song), 22
How She Boogalooed It, 144
Hully Gully, 24, 90, 94, 95
Hushabye, 49

INDEX

I Can Hear Music, 159
I Do, 15, 38
I Get Around, 22, 34, 46, 95, 177
I Just Got My Pay, 55
I Just Wasn't Made For These Times (film), 184
I Just Wasn't Made For These Times (song), 114, 120
I Know There's An Answer, 112
I Shot The Sheriff, 104
I Should Have Known Better, 78, 91
I Was Made To Love Her, 140
I Went To Sleep, 163
I Will Always Love You, 35
I Write The Songs, 161
I'd Love Just Once To See You, 142
I'll Be Home For Christmas, 61
I'm Bugged At My Old Man, 85
I'm So Young, 50, 71, 87
I'm Waiting For The Day, 108
I'm Waiting For The Man, 50
Imagination (Brian Wilson album), 36
In My Childhood, 104
In My Room, 21, 29, 37, 163, 175
In The Back Of My Mind, 74, 114
In The Parkin' Lot, 34
Ingber, Elliot, 18
Inside the Music Of Brian Wilson, 183

Jakobson, Gregg, 169
Jamerson, James, 140
James Bond Theme, 116
Jan and Dean, 10, 14, 19, 26, 27, 64, 68, 96, 174
Jardine, Al, 10, 13, 14, 17, 25, 26, 28, 29, 32, 39, 40, 44, 46, 58, 60, 66, 69, 76, 77, 81, 90, 91, 95, 101, 106, 109, 112, 124, 126, 129, 139, 144, 150–154, 157, 158, 162, 169, 174, 175, 177–182, 184
Jardine, Matt, 44
Jay and The Americans, 67
Jesu, Joy Of Man's Desiring, 81
JFK assassination, 35
Jingle Bells, 59
Johnny B Goode, 32, 177
Johnson, Plas, 65
Johnston, Bruce, 10, 18, 44, 64, 65, 76, 79, 82, 86, 90, 94, 101, 103, 111, 113, 123, 126, 127, 129, 139, 144, 147, 150, 158, 160, 162, 168, 170, 178, 181

Kalinich, Steve, 155, 162
Kaye, Carol, 65, 80, 81, 122
Keep An Eye On Summer, 36
Kessel, Barney, 65
King Midas In Reverse, 139
Kingston Trio, the, 17, 96, 109
Kiss Me Baby, 72
Knechtel, Larry, 122
Kokomo, 104
Korthoff, Steve, 152, 153
Kowalski, Mike, 177, 178

Lady Madonna, 139
Lambert, Philip, 9, 183
Lana, 23
Land Ahoy, 24, 42
Leadbelly, 162
Leaf, David, 147, 152, 154, 185
Leaf, Earl, 75
Lei'd In Hawaii, 147, 158, 182
Lennon, John, 33, 66, 70, 78, 79, 91, 93, 94
Let Him Run Wild, 82, 84, 87
Let The Wind Blow, 143
Let's Go Away For A While, 108
Let's Go Trippin', 23, 176
Little Bird, 154
Little Children, 92
Little Deuce Coupe (album), 25, 39
Little Deuce Coupe (song), 22, 29, 36, 40, 58, 95, 175
Little Girl (You're My Miss America), 16
Little Honda, 46, 49, 53, 55
Little Pad, 134
Little Richard, 52
Little Saint Nick, 53, 58, 59
Live In London, 147, 173, 177
Live Peace In Toronto, 94
Long Tall Texan, 175
Look, Listen, Vibrate, Smile, 183
Lookin' At Tomorrow, 96
Louie (dog), 117
Louie Louie, 37, 54, 79, 154
Louvin Brothers, the, 94
Love Me Do, 15
Love, Darlene, 77, 95
Love, Maureen, 27, 30
Love, Mike, 10, 13–15, 17–24, 26, 27, 29–32, 34–37, 40, 42, 44–47, 49, 51, 52, 54, 56, 58, 59, 61, 66–73, 76, 80–82, 84, 90–93, 95, 100, 101, 103, 105, 106, 108, 109, 112, 113, 119, 121, 123,

125, 126, 129, 133, 135–145, 150–152, 154, 157–162, 167, 171, 174–178, 180–182, 184
   alleged dislike of *Pet Sounds*, 100
   songwriting credit lawsuit, 17, 22, 29, 36, 45, 46, 49, 51, 52, 54, 56, 58, 59, 66, 70, 76–78, 81, 82, 84, 103
LSD, 18, 76, 81, 99, 112
LSD-25 *(Gamblers song)*, 18
Lymon, Frankie & The Teenagers, 36

Maharishi Mahesh Yogi, 154
Mama Says, 145
Manilow, Barry, 16
Manson, Charles, 164, 165
Marcella, 55
Marks, David, 11, 13–15, 18, 19, 26, 39, 40, 184
Marksmen, the, 39
Maybellene, 21
McCartney, Paul, 33, 78, 83, 91, 102
McCoy, Van, 161
Meant For You, 150
Melcher, Terry, 47, 64, 106, 110
Merry Christmas, Baby, 59
Midler, Bette, 66
Migliori, Jay, 65, 122
Miles, Lawrence, 124
Miller, Glenn, 104
Misirlou, 20
Mister Sandman, 132
Mister Tambourine Man, 47
Mitchum, Robert, 32
MOJO Magazine, 34, 64
Moon Dawg, 18
Moonlight Serenade, 105
Morgan, Tommy, 125
Mormonism, 78
Mothers Of Invention, the, 18
Motown, 84
Mountain Of Love, 92
Mrs O'Leary's Cow, 133, 166
Mystics, the, 49

Negron, Chuck, 163
Never Learn Not To Love, 164
Nitzsche, Jack, 77, 85, 115, 154
No-Go Showboat, 43
Noble Surfer, 22
Norberg, Bob, 31, 36
Norman, Monty, 116
Not A Second Time, 79

Not Too Young To Get Married, 50

O'Hagan, Sean, 10
Ol'Man River, 171
Old Folks At Home, 28, 171
Olympics, the, 90
On Wisconsin, 54
Our Car Club, 31, 43
Our Favourite Recording Sessions, 53
Our Prayer, 165

Pacific Ocean Blue (album), 12
Paley, Andy, 10
Palisades Park, 15, 27, 76
Palmer, Earl, 65
Papa-Oom-Mow-Mow, 55, 92, 176
Paperback Writer, 109
Parks, Jon, 152, 153
Parks, Van Dyke, 127, 129, 132, 133, 135, 136, 165, 167, 184
Passing By, 153, 156
Peaches, 52
Penny Lane, 102
Pet Sounds (album), 10, 28, 45, 58, 65, 66, 75, 85, 87, 89, 99, 101, 103, 106, 107, 109, 114, 120, 127, 178, 179
Pet Sounds (song), 83, 115
Philles records, 159
Pinetop's Boogie Woogie, 31
Pitman, Bill, 102
Planet Of Giants, 124
Please Let Me Wonder, 66, 70, 71
Please Mister Postman, 35
Pohlman, Ray, 65, 122
Pom Pom Play Girl, 36, 79
Pomus, Doc, 49
Presley, Elvis, 52, 139
Priore, Domenic, 183

Ramones, the, 66
Randi, Don, 65, 110, 115
Reagan, Ronald, 170
Redwood, 142, 163
Regents, the, 96
REM, 115
Revolver, 83
Reynolds, Dick, 57, 60, 61
Rhapsody In Blue, 60, 104
Richard, Cliff, 66
Riddle, Nelson, 60
Ride The Wild Surf, 19
Rimsky-Korsakov, Nikolai, 31

INDEX

Rip-Chords, the, 64
Ritz, Lyle, 65, 81, 157
Rivers, Johnny, 92
Rivingtons, the, 92, 176
Robbins, Marty, 130
Robinson, William "Smokey", 79
Rock and Roll (Tom Stoppard play), 149
Rolling Stone (magazine), 64
Ronettes, the, 33, 71, 159
Ross, Diana, 67
Rovell, Barbara, 68
Rovell, Diane, 54, 68, 110
Rubber Soul, 99
Run, James, Run, 116
Russell, Leon, 65

Sachen, Terry, 112
Sail On, Sailor, 139
Salt Lake City, 69, 78
Salt Lake City (city in Utah), 32, 78
San Francisco (Flowers In Your Hair), 139
Santa Claus Is Coming To Town, 61
Santa's Beard, 59
Save The Last Dance For Me, 130
sexism, 19, 36, 40, 52, 55, 79, 81, 82, 153
Sgt Pepper's Lonely Hearts Club Band (the Beatles album), 112
Sharon Marie, 141
Shaw, Artie, 105
She Knows Me Too Well, 59, 73
She's Goin' Bald, 133
She's Leaving Home, 137
Shortenin' Bread, 70, 148
Shuman, Mort, 49
Shut Down, 21, 37, 42
Shut Down (compilation album), 32
Shut Down Part II, 37
Shut Down Vol. 2, 25, 31, 45
Sidewalk Surfin', 27
Silhouettes, the, 134
Simon and Garfunkel, 94
Sloan, P.F., 96
Sloop John B, 96, 100, 104, 109, 131, 179
Smile, 10, 55, 117, 127, 129, 131–133, 135, 137, 138, 143, 145, 148, 155, 157, 159, 165, 171
Smiley Smile, 106, 119, 127–129, 132–138, 141, 147, 182
Smokey Bear, 53
Something, 71
South Bay Surfer, 28

Spector, Phil, 10, 27, 38, 46, 49, 50, 53, 61, 65, 67, 71, 77, 85, 86, 95, 130, 159
Spector, Veronica "Ronnie", 50, 71
Spirit Of America, 43
Stack O' Tracks, 83, 89
Stars And Stripes Vol. 1, 175
Stebbins, Jon, 184
Stoked, 20
Stoppard, Tom, 149
Strange, Billy, 65
Stranglers, the, 52
Strzelecki, Henry, 175
Sugar Sugar, 16
Summer Days... And Summer Nights, 45, 63–65, 75, 99, 103
Summer Days... And Summer Nights, 135, 177
Summer Means New Love, 84
Summertime Blues, 18
Sunflower, 87, 162, 170
Supernaw, Doug, 175
Supremes, the, 67
Surf City, 14, 19, 64
Surf Finger, 115
Surf Jam, 23
Surf's Up (song), 129
Surfaris, the, 23
Surfer Girl (album), 25, 39, 40, 43
Surfer Girl (song), 19, 21, 26, 28, 29, 35, 38, 52
Surfers Rule, 30
Surfin', 13, 14, 17, 158
Surfin' Down The Swanee River, 28
Surfin' Safari (album), 13, 14, 42, 76
Surfin' Safari (song), 14–16, 26
Surfin' USA (album), 13, 19, 24, 42
Surfin' USA (song), 19, 21, 77
Survivors, the, 41
Swanee Kazoo, 49
Sweet Little Sixteen, 20
Swift, Jonathan, 134

Tanner, Paul, 124, 139
Tears On My Pillow, 50
Tedesco, Tommy, 65
Tell Me Why, 78, 91
Ten Little Indians, 15
That Means A Lot, 78
That's Not Me, 106, 113
The Baker Man, 24
The Beach Boys Love You, 128, 149

The Beach Boys Today, 28, 45, 57, 63–65, 73, 75, 80, 177
The Beach Boys' Christmas Album, 57, 66, 69
The Boy From New York City, 76, 123
The Captain And Tenneille, 178
The Complete Guide To The Music Of The Beach Boys, 183
The Girl From New York City, 76, 84, 123
The Hustle, 161
The Lady's Dressing Room, 134
The Little Girl I Once Knew, 55, 86, 117
The Little Old Lady From Pasadena, 174
The Locomotion, 24
The Lonely Sea, 21, 26
The Lonely Surfer, 85, 115
The Lost Beach Boy, 184
The Lost Concert, 174, 175
The Man With All The Toys, 59
The Monster Mash, 95, 176
The Nearest Faraway Place, 161, 162
The Pet Sounds Sessions (box set), 101, 107, 111, 113
The Rocking Surfer, 28
The Shift, 19, 23
The Smile Sessions, 127
The Surfer Moon, 28, 31, 40
The Survivors, 73
The Times They Are A-Changin', 95
The Wanderer, 93, 176
The Warmth Of The Sun, 35
the White Album (Beatles album), 154
Their Hearts Were Full Of Spring, 44, 147, 181
Them, 143
Theme From A Broken Heart, 85
Then I Kissed Her, 77
There's No Other (Like My Baby), 95
Things Are Changing For The Better, 67
Thinkin' 'Bout You, Baby, 141
This Boy, 35
This Car Of Mine, 36
Thomas, Joe, 10
Three Dog Night, 142, 163
Ticket To Ride, 78, 79, 81
Time To Get Alone, 163
Tobler, John, 183
Torrence, Dean, 90, 96, 182
Transcendental Meditation, 150, 157
Trombone Dixie, 117
Troup, Bobby, 44, 147
Turner, Ike and Tina, 130

U.S. Male, 139
Ultimate Christmas, 53, 58
Underwater, 158
Usher, Gary, 15, 16, 18, 21, 29, 36, 38, 50

Vail, Fred, 174
Vegetables, 132, 145
Velvet Underground, the, 49
Venet, Nik, 15, 18
Vescovo, Al, 157
von Otter, Anne Sofie, 107

Wake The World, 151, 180
Walk Like A Man, 30
Walk On By, 170
Walking In The Rain, 33
Was, Don, 184
We Three Kings Of Orient Are, 60
We'll Run Away, 50, 71
We're Together Again, 170
Weaver, Derry, 18
Weavers, the, 109
Wechter, Julius, 65
Wendy, 51
When A Man Needs A Woman, 153, 154
When I Grow Up (To Be A Man), 68
When You Wish Upon A Star, 26
Whistle In, 138
White Christmas, 61
White Light/White Heat, 50
White, Jack, 139
Why Do Fools Fall In Love?, 36
Why Don't They Let Us Fall In Love, 50
Wilcock, Alex, 108
Wild Honey (album), 89, 120, 127, 136, 138–145, 147
Wild Honey (song), 139
Willis, Wesley, 11
Wilson, Brian, 9, 12–15, 17–38, 40–43, 45, 46, 48–52, 54–61, 63, 65–86, 90–93, 95, 96, 99, 101, 102, 104, 106, 108–112, 114, 116, 117, 120, 123, 124, 126–129, 131–136, 138–145, 147, 149–159, 162, 163, 165, 168–171, 174, 176–182, 184
  marriage to Marilyn Rovell, 63, 99
  mental health problems, 63, 99, 127, 168
  stops touring, 64, 99
Wilson, Carl, 10, 12–15, 18–20, 22, 23, 26, 28, 32, 36, 37, 40, 44, 46, 51, 55, 58, 65–67, 69, 70, 76,

INDEX 193

    79, 90–92, 96, 101, 106, 111, 122, 124–126, 129, 134, 135, 137, 139–142, 144, 150–152, 155, 158–160, 163, 165, 170, 174, 178–181, 184

Wilson, Carnie, 153

Wilson, Dennis, 10, 12–14, 16, 19, 26, 30, 32, 36, 37, 40, 41, 46, 47, 52, 61, 66–68, 73–76, 90, 93, 96, 101, 106, 113, 114, 125–127, 129, 135, 139, 150, 152–155, 158, 161, 164, 166, 169, 170, 174–176, 178, 184

Wilson, Marilyn, 33, 54, 68, 75, 90, 91, 108, 110, 153
    marriage to Brian Wilson, 63

Wilson, Murry, 17, 26, 39, 116, 168

Wilson, Ron (Surfari), 23

Wilson, Ron (We're Together Again writer), 170

Wind Chimes, 135

Wipe Out, 23

With Me Tonight, 69, 135

Wonder, Stevie, 140

Wonderful, 116, 129, 136

Wood, Tat, 124

Woody Woodpecker, 133

Wouldn't It Be Nice, 17, 100, 102, 104, 117, 179

Wrecking Crew, the, 65

You Can't Catch Me, 21

You Still Believe In Me, 104, 107

You're So Good To Me, 84

You're Welcome, 146

You've Got To Hide Your Love Away, 78, 93, 95

Your Summer Dream, 31, 40

Zappa, Frank, 37, 94, 132

Zelig, 94

Made in the USA
Las Vegas, NV
16 April 2022